PRAISE FOR *CULTIVATE*

"*Cultivate* provides an honest look at the importance of teamwork and how it drives the success of your business."

Jeff Penz
Choctaw Casino & Resort Senior Director of Gaming

"My dad would often say 'You are dependent on others, so others must be dependent on you.' A winning team depends on both the team and you; *Cultivate* has made this easy to digest, understand, and win!"

John Miller
CEO
Denny's Inc.

"This book is a quick and highly entertaining read, full of pragmatic and insightful lessons on everyday leadership. A great reminder to always put people and purpose first!"

Kelly Baker
Executive Vice President & Chief Human Resources Officer
Thrivent Financial

"Anyone can win once; only teams that are built with intention and tenacity become champions. *Cultivate* has captured the DNA of championship teams."

Anton Vincent
President,
Mars Wrigley, North America

"Teamwork is how I see the world. *Cultivate* nailed the very essence of how winning teams should operate. Congrats, Walter and team. You nailed it!"

Kevin McHale
NBA Hall of Fame
Boston Celtics

"*Cultivate* is a must-read book for any leader who wants a straightforward formula to learn how to build a better team to get better results. *Cultivate* introduces the reader to three college friends, Alex, Bobbie, and Collin, who reunite on the golf course and are joined by Alex's daughter Austin, a rising college freshman. Over a competitive game of golf, they discuss their business and personal successes and challenges, while Alex manages to weave his wisdom as to the six key attributes of a successful team into the conversation in a fun, quirky, and easily readable format."

"Alex's ability to artfully impart his knowledge and advice, combined with his enthusiasm and skill for teaching and mentoring, are good reminders that the best leaders are able to *cultivate* other leaders!"

Diana Garvis Purcel
Independent Board Member and
Former Chief Financial Officer

cultivate

WALTER BOND AND **ANTOINETTE BOND**

cultivate

THE SIX
NON-NEGOTIABLE TRAITS
OF A
WINNING TEAM

WILEY

Published by John Wiley & Sons, Inc., Hoboken, New Jersey.
Published simultaneously in Canada.

For general information on our other products and services or for technical support, please contact our Customer Care Department within the United States at (800) 762-2974, outside the United States at (317) 572-3993 or fax (317) 572-4002.

Wiley also publishes its books in a variety of electronic formats. Some content that appears in print may not be available in electronic formats. For more information about Wiley products, visit our web site at www.wiley.com.

Library of Congress Cataloging-in-Publication Data:

Names: Bond, Walter, 1969- author. | Bond, Antoinette, author.
Title: Cultivate : the six non-negotiable traits of a winning team : a
  business fable / Walter Bond and Antoinette Bond.
Description: Hoboken, New Jersey : John Wiley & Sons, Inc., [2023]
Identifiers: LCCN 2022033469 (print) | LCCN 2022033470 (ebook) | ISBN
  9781119909118 (cloth) | ISBN 9781119909125 (adobe pdf) | ISBN
  9781119909132 (epub)
Subjects: LCSH: Teams in the workplace—Management. | Organizational
  behavior. | Organizational effectiveness. | Corporate culture. |
  Leadership.
Classification: LCC HD66 .B6538 2023 (print) | LCC HD66 (ebook) | DDC
  658.4/022—dc23/eng/20220729
LC record available at https://lccn.loc.gov/2022033469
LC ebook record available at https://lccn.loc.gov/2022033470

COVER ART & DESIGN: PAUL MCCARTHY

SKY10044059_030623

Contents

PREFACE

Discover The 6 Secrets to Build a Championship-Caliber Team That Can Outperform Your Competition, Plus Achieve Goals You May Think Are Impossible Today

If your company or organization wants to get to the next level of success, you'll need to cultivate a team mindset among each of your employees.

Using the proven ideas and concepts in their new book *Cultivate*, Walter Bond and Antoinette Bond provide the insight into how you and your teammates can improve your team performance and to become a champion in your industry and sustain a competitive advantage.

Walter and Antoinette highlight the six non-negotiable traits of a winning team through a business fable. The fable contains characters that resemble real-life people you can identify with as they encounter challenging situations and make breakthrough achievements, especially when they work as a team to accomplish a common goal.

By improving on the team skills illustrated throughout the book, you can learn to become a peak team performer who is able to achieve bigger goals than you might otherwise attain by yourself.

Many companies and organizations today are struggling to hire, develop, and retain top talent. Moreover, many managerial leaders fail to recognize they have a teamwork problem, and even fewer know how to improve teamwork.

That's why Walter and Antoinette have written this book. It fulfills an unmet need among entrepreneurs, executives, and managers in a variety of industries.

Good teamwork leads to greater success. By applying the ideas, concepts, and skills communicated throughout the book, you can turn your company or organization into a champion-caliber, peak-performing team that can dominate your industry.

Ready to get started?

FOREWORD

FIRST IMPRESSION THAT HAS LASTED TO THIS DAY. . .

I first met Walter Bond in early 2013 when Jersey Mike's agreed to be part of an episode of a Food Network series called *Giving You the Business*. Walter was the host of the show.

After sharing our respective backgrounds and filming the show, I knew Walter would help our company going forward. Soon after, I asked Walter to join our Jersey Mike's National Conference as a guest keynote speaker.

WALTER ELECTRIFIED OUR AUDIENCE WHEREVER HE SPOKE. . .

Walter came on the stage and had an unbelievable presence. He captured the crowd immediately and received a thundering standing ovation.

After that, Walter spoke at two other national meetings and several leadership meetings that were held with owners, area directors, and their managers. He continued to teach us how to recruit, develop, and retain top people so that we could stand apart from our competitors.

Walter got our employees to understand our goals, adopt our company culture, work as a team, and express excellence.

SIX YEARS LATER. . .OUR BOLDEST DECISION IN COMPANY HISTORY

Six years later I called Walter and his wife and business partner Antoinette to invite them to join me in our company's biggest initiative ever—to do something never done before in the history of franchising. Walter immediately said yes!

I asked Walter how we should communicate the message he was teaching throughout our national organization of franchisees. Like a true coach, Walter said to me, "Peter, that's easy. Just be you, and tell them what is in your heart and what you want to do and why."

Walter, Antoinette, Tatiana, and I traveled to more than 25 cities together across the United States. He made a big impact among our team in each location. In the end, the owners of each franchise saw us as true partners with them.

It was a pivotal moment in the history of our company that we will never forget. Spending so many days and nights together on the road with Walter to deliver the message of unity to our teams and crews across the nation was truly inspiring.

As we look back on these initiatives, our investment was a key building block to launch forward like never before. Today we stand as one of the top franchise systems in the country.

OUR POST-COVID GOALS ARE COMING TO FRUITION, THANKS TO WALTER BOND AND HIS NEW BOOK

Now, after COVID, we're ready again to have meetings and gatherings with everyone throughout our system across the country. Walter, Antoinette, my wife Tatiana, and I will be traveling across the country. They will meet with our owners, managers, and our teams to motivate us to stay on track with our mission. Then we'll finish our journey with our long-awaited national meeting.

I'm especially excited that on this road trip we will bring the development principles from Walter and Antionette's new book *Cultivate*.

The book has many active examples that show how best to manage our day-to-day lives and what path we should choose to take. Walter will motivate, teach, and coach our team. He'll help us communicate our plan and help us understand the goal and the path ahead.

Cultivate reminds us to step back and check on how we are doing. For me, it was to take another look at our mission statement as a company. To give and make a difference in someone's life. To help raise people up together with the mindset to provide service to others.

While those may sound like words, this book shows how we can turn those words into action that produces results.

After reading *Cultivate*, I can honestly say, "Yes, we are staying true to ourselves, and we are re-inspired!"

IT IS TIME TO "CULTIVATE." I hope you enjoy reading the book and execute what you'll learn.

Peter Cancro, Founder and CEO,
Jersey Mike's Subs

ACKNOWLEDGMENTS

Kelly Baker, we'd like to thank you for your invaluable insight as we began the journey to advance our vision of teamwork and how it relates to maximizing human capital and building stronger teams. Our conversations have really cemented what great teams look like on a C-suite level.

Daniel Grissom, thank you for your partnership as we honed in and defined the traits that make successful teams click.

Peter Cancro, a big thank-you to you and the entire Jersey Mike's Subs team. Our partnership has helped us see what great teamwork and culture look like up close. You have set a high standard of what is possible through cooperation.

Golf Savants: We want to thank Chris Zeller, Paul Clivio, Corey Robert Davis, Andy Bush, and Samuel Puryear for your input on golf. When you're not a golfer yourself and write a book using golf as the backdrop, you had better call in the real professionals for help and guidance.

The Bond Group team: Thank you to our team members who continually help us push our company and projects forward. Kendall Bond, Justin Greiman, Diana McCarthy, Jeff Traister, Steven Van Tassell, Amy Wirth, Kirsten Womack, and Abir Zayed are invaluable to our current and future success. You already know this, but we'll tell you anyway: we cannot do anything without you.

CULTIVATE VERB

cul·ti·vate | \ ˈkəl-tə-ˌvāt

TO IMPROVE BY LABOR, CARE, OR STUDY :

We believe that all great teams have similar characteristics and traits. Six traits are non-negotiable for a winning organization to operate at a high level (see Figure I.1). *Cultivate* is designed to be the go-to guide for employees and employers who want to build a high-performing corporate team or be part of one. Impact players who work together harmoniously make up the core of successful, elite teams.

It sounds simple, yet many organizations struggle with it. This book offers readers a practical, applicable guide to recruiting, developing, and retaining qualified employees to build powerhouse organizations through the eyes of relatable characters in our story.

When you meet Alex and shake his hand, you may do a double-take. You may see a reflection of yourself.

6 NON-NEGOTIABLE TRAITS

COMMON GOALS	COMMUNICATION	ACCOUNTABILITY
A winning team requires everyone focused and working toward the same goal together. Your goal needs to be clear and concise with buy-in and agreement from everyone.	A winning team requires up-front, open, and honest communication with no hidden agendas. If something is not right, talk about it right away.	A winning team must consist of teammates who can own up to and admit mistakes without blaming others. Ownership starts at the top.
TRUST	**CHEMISTRY**	**COMMITMENT**
A winning team is built on transparency and absolute faith in your teammate's abilities and motives. Trust is strongest when everyone values and depends on one another to play their role with complete confidence in one another.	A winning team requires a collection of diverse skillsets and abilities with like-minded individuals creating the perfect synergy. Talent is maximized to leverage everyone's skills for the good of the team.	A winning team consists of members who are completely devoted emotionally and intellectually. Because team members know why they are there and how they can help advance the cause, they are locked in and willing to do what is necessary to achieve the desired results.

Figure I.1 The six non-negotiable traits

Alex started with one store, probably like you, and grew it into a much larger company. Early on Alex spent his weekends working and nurturing his company, but now his weekends are spent on his family. Alex loves people. They're the most critical thing in the world to him. He made the company office feel like a home-away-from-home for the enjoyment of his teammates—his work family. Alex loves face-to-face meetings, believing it helps his team stay connected. Alex is in the people business.

Maybe you'll identify more with Bobbi, aka the Energizer Bunny. Bobbi is a micromanager, with an emphasis on the micro. There are no details too small for her attention. She is happiest when she has multiple projects running, making her employees into extensions of herself to accomplish much more than one person alone can.

You might see yourself in Collin, although we hope not. Collin is unable to admit his shortcomings. It's always someone else's fault. He had all the platitudes to accompany his business personality: "It's not our job to hold their hands. We are not their friends. It's not personal." Collin's problem is that he always hires guys just like him.

Alex learned how to run a successful business as a teenager working for Mr. Hank, a neighbor with a landscaping business. From Mr. Hank, Alex learned how to cultivate a successful enterprise and the traits it needs to grow. At first, he didn't know it, but he was learning about establishing common goals, communicating effectively, and finding the chemistry necessary to bring together a diverse yet successful team. Most important, he learned about the lifeblood of a business: commitment, accountability, and trust.

As you read this book, we'll prompt you with reflections about what you've read and the actions you need to take for your business's success. We hope you'll let these lessons sink deep into your soil and take root, helping you grow and improve.

1

"A" GAME

Alex checked his reflection in the full-size mirror by the front door one more time. He couldn't remember exactly when the navy blue sports coat and white dress shirt became his uniform, but it has become his signature look, and it suited him well. The look always reminded Alex of how far he had come. He headed outside, and his Tesla reacted as he got closer to the car. He settled into the driver's seat and reversed down the long stone driveway, wove through the perfectly manicured streets of his gated community, and waved at Gertie at the guard gate before turning onto the main road. He always says hi to everyone, whether a resident or a worker, rich or poor. Alex believed that you shouldn't just communicate with people; you should *connect* with everyone. The most important thing in the world to Alex is people.

Years ago, when he was looking for office space, two things were important to him. One was being close to home, which benefited him and his family, and two was that it had a lot of windows that benefited his teammates at work. He wanted his culture to feel open and free so everyone could enjoy working together and enjoy life. Alex devoted his day to taking care of all his *people*. The office on Gardner Street was the perfect fit. The open-concept space featured exposed brick walls, trendy lounge furniture in the center, and private offices and conference rooms settled behind floor-to-ceiling glass walls. The laptop-friendly workstations built into the wall and designed to look like classic workbenches were Alex's favorite feature.

He wanted his office to feel like a really cool home-away-from-home for all his teammates to enjoy.

It was Saturday morning, so the office was quieter and slower than usual, but there were still a few people buzzing around the space. He didn't ever have to ask anyone to work extra, come in early, or work weekends. Everyone sort of did this on their own. It was part of the culture from day one. Everyone, for the most part, was completely dialed in and connected to the business. Alex built an amazing business from humble beginnings using some simple but non-negotiable strategies.

Alex walked into the first conference room and checked his watch—8:30 a.m. All his regional managers would arrive in the next hour. Alex was a simple man and found security being where he needed to be long before anyone else. He wanted that to bleed through his culture. He was a stickler for time. *On time is late, and early is on time* was his favorite mantra. He paced the room, carefully pushing in the chairs, adjusting the table slightly, and checking his reflection again in the large window overlooking the parking lot.

Alex believed in meetings. He didn't believe in long meetings, but he believed in getting the team together as much as he could face-to-face. He loved Zoom too if it meant his team could talk and stay connected. But his face-to-face meetings were his favorite, and he didn't mind the extra expense; he thought it was well worth it.

All of his meetings were run the same way on purpose and didn't involve a lot of preparation. Everyone knew the basic template. Alex didn't like surprises, so his meetings were run very efficiently, and the rhythm of them was predictable. His regional managers grew to love the predictability of his meetings and knew the flow very well. Everything was mapped out, and every regional manager knew the expectation of how to run their region. These meetings could practically run themselves.

Alex started with one store but now owned 150 stores with 2,000 employees that brought in more than $300 million in revenue. He believed each store needed its own dedicated crew of about 12–15 people. The goal was to build a perfectly constructed team that operated at a championship level. The *crew* was what made each store tick. This meeting with his 16 regional managers was everything to Alex. Each regional manager had the task of recruiting, developing, and retaining top talent and building each crew at each store they managed. It was the only meeting he ran himself. This one was his pride and joy, and he felt it was his most critical meeting to keep his team and culture strong and positioned for growth.

He looked up when he heard a knock at the conference room door. Two tiny, uniformed women with large rolling carts stood smiling in the doorway. He ushered them in and helped them set up the goodies in the middle of the table. Two boxes of bagels, two dozen donuts, three trays of muffins, three portable cardboard containers filled with black coffee, a few flavored creamers, napkins, plates, and two bowls of assorted fruits. He looked at the table and hoped it would be enough for the 16 attendees; he always struggled with estimating how much he'd need for events like this. Alex had placed the order with the local breakfast cafe the night before with special instructions to have it delivered by 9:15 a.m. and "don't forget the vegan and the gluten-free people!"

He tipped the women generously and went about setting up the breakfast foods in a precise and organized manner. After a few minutes of rearranging the food on the table, the first wave of regional managers began to arrive. Ben from region 3 and Carla from region 4 walked in and greeted Alex with firm handshakes and a smile.

Alex, known for his simple but powerful ideas, created a way to differentiate their stores from any other brand and each store from another. He created a numbering system where he classified each region based on the sequence of when the store opened. The lower the region number, the longer it's been open.

The others arrived quickly after, and the conference room began buzzing with quiet conversations. Alex loved it. He would join in and chit-chat often but just loved to observe his work family coming together. Everyone helped themselves to plates loaded with breakfast treats and found their seat around the conference table. Alex looked around at his team of regional managers and felt a sense of pride. The co-leaders and teammates of his winning team had arrived.

Everyone was happy, smiling, and interacting with each other, just like it was a family reunion. Culture, his people, and team pride were everything to Alex. He let them connect for as long as possible and then brought the meeting to order. Alex believed the time to connect with your peers socially was critical to the brand, and although he never said it publicly, he thought it was the most important part of the meeting.

He kept his meeting short because the real reunion would happen after the regional meeting at the bar located right across the street from the office. The bar loved Alex, and Alex loved the bar. He kept a running tab, and his team could just sign for the drinks or food, and the bar billed Alex once a month. It was just another small detail that made Alex lovable to his teammates. He was the employer of choice, and it was easy to see why once you joined Alex and his team, you were a teammate for life. He was always looking for ways to take care of his people.

Almost 20 years ago, he had taken a chance and invested his life savings, his very last dime, into a hardware store in the quaint downtown area near his home in San Jose. That was store 1. Now, Alex was the owner of 150 stores around the region and took pride in hiring the best of the best to run each location. Alex took it upon himself to recruit and select each regional manager himself.

He knew these hires were his most critical hires, they needed to be the right kind of leader with the right kind of heart. His company was known as a dream job and routinely found a place on the "Best Places to Work" list in almost every business publication.

He loved telling the story about how he was writing his business plan and had to come up with a name for this hardware store he never knew he was going to start. He tossed around a ton of ideas, but nothing seemed to fit. And then, when he couldn't possibly think anymore and needed to walk away from it for a bit, he tossed his shirt into the dirty hamper and was getting ready to jump in the shower. He looked quickly at his reflection, and his eyes shot directly to the tattoo of a redwood on his arm. It was a tribute to his mentor, Mr. Hank. There was a meaning and a story behind the redwood tree, and Alex got the tattoo on the first anniversary of Mr. Hank's death. Redwood Hardware, Alex decided. *Perfect.* Over time, the chain became known as Red's throughout the community, but the story and meaning behind the name were always very special to Alex.

Alex believed in "owners" and that everyone who works for him should own something. Alex always said, "Owners stay longer than renters." He decided against the franchise model, but every one of his regional managers and store managers share in the profits. It had been a while since he brought all of his regional store managers together, but before he went on vacation, he wanted to get them together to express his gratitude for their hard work over the last year and create a space for authentic conversation, as well as feedback, questions, and concerns. Alex was thrilled with where business was now, but the vision was for a national footprint, so he couldn't afford to become complacent.

Alex believed in slow and steady growth just like a tree. He believed that if you planted it in the perfect place, it would thrive, and if you nurtured it, it would grow big and strong and reach its full potential. In the beginning, you are taking care of the tree, and soon enough the tree will be taking care of you.

Once he had this region the way he wanted, Alex believed the whole country was their next feat. Alex would always say, "Business is just like a tree; you need slow and steady growth."

Everyone knew that Alex was always quoting this phrase. He got the nickname Tree Boy around the office because he was always using analogies around landscaping, flowers, and gardening. It all started when Christy made a surprise visit to the store and accidentally called him one of her favorite nicknames, Tree Boy. Shawn had heard the endearing nickname, and Alex knew it was over. By the end of the day, all of his teammates were using the nickname. He pretended to hate it, but deep down he loved it.

In the beginning, nobody remembers exactly when, but Alex spent weeks in his work shed creating a masterpiece. He put hours of blood, sweat, and tears into his craft, and the end result was a gorgeous, handcrafted sign made out of redwood that said,

"We are not in the hardware business, we are in the people business."

Now, as a tradition for each new store, that original sign is flown to the new location and hung in the back office by Alex himself before anyone is hired.

Alex wasn't ashamed of the fact that he always had tears streaming down his face as he hung the original sign. Red's Hardware has a great reputation in the industry. Some industry experts call it a cult. Alex initially was very uncomfortable with that language, but he later understood that it was intended to be a compliment. Now, Alex jokes that the root word of *culture* is *cult*!

In the early days, Christy and Alex ran the store and built the foundation together. Christy always ran the books and was in charge of the numbers. But working together caused some serious problems for them as a couple. Christy was always stressed out, and Alex was learning how to lead. Alex learned after a few years that his business will always be a reflection of him. If he wants his business to grow, he must grow first. When they were ready, they hired Shawn.

Alex remembered the tall, extremely shy, lanky, nerdy college kid walking in for an application, and Alex wasn't so sure he'd be the right fit at first. Christy loved him right away as he had a background in math. She also had a more personal reason for wanting to get Shawn on board as soon as possible: Shawn would be her replacement, and she knew that when he was hired, she could step back and step into the role she desired. As an only child, having a large family was very important to her. This was Alex's baby, not hers. Alex saw potential in Shawn and immediately went to work developing and cultivating his confidence. As a former college golfer, Alex knew that confidence was the difference in his teammate's performance.

Shawn was a numbers guy. He was a quick thinker, was great at mental math, and had a very analytical brain. Over time, Alex would learn that when there were numbers to crunch, P&L reports to read, or accounts to be balanced, Shawn was the guy. Initially, Alex hired Shawn because he knew that Shawn was strong in areas that Alex was not. As Shawn learned more about the company, he mimicked and mirrored the way Alex interacted with people, and soon it became contagious. Alex would always preach to Shawn, "We are in the people business, Shawn!" Shawn bought in from day one and became a pillar on the team.

Alex opened the meeting as he always did, with a statement as everyone chimed in. "We are not in the hardware business, we are in the people business." Then he went on by expressing gratitude for their hard work and reporting on some of the highlights of each store. This meeting was not about facts and figures, but about really listening to the needs and concerns of his team. He then effortlessly flowed into listing the company's key performance indicators and asked for feedback on the new technology and software that was being implemented in some of the stores. He paid special attention to his regional managers who had just been promoted to make sure they were executing "The Red's Hardware Way."

After quickly reviewing the store's safety and security guidelines, the best part of the meeting began: the open-ended conversations. Alex wanted to hear some good news about each store: "Always give me some good news first." One by one, each regional manager gave a positive report about their region and each store. The open-ended conversation was critical because each regional manager would alert Alex of what they needed or what problem they needed taken away.

As CEO, his number-one focus was not what his regional managers could do for him but, rather, what he could do for his regional managers. Alex knew that if he served these 16 professionals well, his entire organization would run like a well-oiled machine.

Although Alex saw the world as a master landscaper and gardener, there was one tool he despised: the machete. He taught his regional managers, "You can't walk around with a machete all day tearing your people down. A machete is a tool used when you have lots of things to cut. We are coaches, and coaches walk around with a whistle instead.

We build our crews up. We don't cut down. Sometimes we have to gently prune, but it is to promote growth."

Once the meeting transitioned to the conversation, Alex was all ears, and he and Shawn took copious notes to make sure he gave his regional managers exactly what they needed.

Aside from the amazing financial benefit, they knew they mattered and were important to the brand. His culture was cult-like: everyone had the same mindset, and Alex had duplicated himself through his leadership and therefore built an amazing culture. But everyone was allowed their freedom at the same time. When you were ever confused about what to do or even in doubt, the question became, WWAD. What would Alex do? And all of a sudden, the answer was clear.

Tyesha had an idea of how one of her stores could participate in the town's annual community cleanup, Joe vented his frustrations about the company's cumbersome return policy, and Greg proposed an idea of hosting weekend workshops where kids could come and learn to use specific tools or build things like birdhouses. Alex wanted them to be transparent and speak their mind. As the room buzzed with conversation, Alex listened closely and used his iPad to jot down notes and ideas. If an idea was good and could help the business, Alex would act immediately and give the proper credit to the creator of the idea. His teammates knew that Alex listened to his people. Alex believed in a de-layered organizational structure. "There is no Big I and a little you. Redwood Hardware is about us," he would say.

Alex was the undeniable leader, but these regional managers knew they helped build this thing too. When the room quieted down, Alex asked each regional manager how they were serving their communities. Each store had to be involved in its community and be philanthropic, but he left it up to the regional and store managers how they'd contribute to their individual communities. "If you own something, you stay longer than if you rent."

Alex knew that although each store must have the same culture, he left the product mix up to each regional and store managers because he trusted his leaders to know what people buy in their area. Each regional manager was responsible for overseeing 8–10 stores each and ran their meetings with the same simple template that Alex used. The idea was that if they all ran their meetings the same way Alex ran his meetings, the culture should bleed down to each store.

"Tell me about your crews. Tell me about the managers who are running the stores daily. Are you noticing any issues or obstacles?" He knew the key for a strong culture was for his regional managers to care for their people the same way Alex cared for them. He even allowed each regional manager to run a tab at a local bar and offer their crews a place to hang out. And the regional managers took care of the bill. Shawn paid attention to this bill, because he and Alex knew from experience, the larger the bill, the stronger the crew.

"Are you making sure your new hires are onboarded to the crew in the right way? What practices have you put in place to help your team understand our common goals?" Alex asked these questions every time and appreciated that his regional managers came prepared with a response. These regional managers were his hires, and he looked for professionals who were likable and knew how to motivate and inspire others.

Carlos shared with the group that some of his managers have been having one-on-one meetings with each of the teammates and defining goals using the SMART methodology. Jen, one of the newer managers, mentioned that one of her 10 stores was starting to struggle after one of her managers hired a toxic employee who quickly and drastically altered the company culture in just the few short weeks since she started. She candidly asked around the table for ideas and suggestions on how to help her store manager build the trust back in their team. Alex and the team reminded her about the differences between a company with a high level of trust versus a low level of trust. It was like one voice; they all got it and believed the same things.

It was important for Jen to communicate with more experienced regional managers, especially with Alex present.

In a strong family, the older kids modeled good behavior because they knew the younger kids were looking up to them. Alex just watched as his seasoned regional managers began to coach Jen on the impact and what to do to fix a bad situation.

He would just listen like a proud papa, as his older regional managers helped mentor and coach the younger regional managers. Sometimes Alex would get emotional as the gravity of what Red's Hardware had become hit him. When the seasoned ones are stepping in to teach the new ones, that is when you know you have a strong culture.

The final recommendation was that when there are trust issues between teammates, the overall energy of the business decreases, and so does productivity.

"A low-trust organization produces highly stressed environments, which is never good for business," Alex reminded her seriously. He repeated exactly what his regional managers had to say but shifted the conversation to an in-depth talk about accountability in the workplace, transparency, and Jen's ability to help rebuild this trust with intentionality.

"We are in the people business, and we love our people, Jen. I've seen how you love your people. But we can do that to a fault. We can't afford to allow one person to destroy what we built. What *you* built! A bad fit should be obvious. What happens at your store happens to all of us. I hate firing people. I hate those meetings where we had to let people go too, but they were necessary. The best part of having a strong culture is that bad fits are obvious."

Alex knew what Jen needed to do, but he had the patience and self-control to allow her to come to her own obvious conclusion. Alex needed Jen to own it. Alex learned years ago that to grow and increase capacity he couldn't get into the short grass, and he surely can't micromanage.

Alex offered a final word: "Sometimes people are toxic because they are toxic, but I've learned some people have some personal things going on, and that is what makes them toxic. Jen, you need to find out what is going on with your crew member who may be hurting outside of work. Be decisive based on what you learn."

"What about the chemistry in your stores?" Alex asked, looking around the room. He listened carefully for words like *collaboration, execution, quick shifts, creative thinking, big-picture thinking, detail orientation*, and *interpersonal skills*. From what he was hearing, it seemed like his regional managers were taking the time to hire managers and build teams to fit with the company culture and to add to the chemistry of the store. "Don't grab random people; they must fit the culture, and everyone must complement each other's skill set. If we are in the people business, hire good people." Alex reminded them. *A beautiful landscape is made up of all types of vegetation, and they work together perfectly.* And so should your crew.

"Experience is not always a good thing. Sometimes it's hard for people to unlearn their bad habits. Hire for attitude and train for skill," Shawn chimed in.

Alex always asked the same questions at each meeting so his regional managers knew what was important to Alex and the success of the business. He always focused on the six non-negotiable traits of a winning team. He believed if his stores mastered these six things, their stores would be unstoppable. Everyone knew these six traits were their responsibility to cultivate:

1. Common goal
2. Communication
3. Accountability
4. Trust
5. Chemistry
6. Commitment

He closed out the meeting by reminding each regional manager that they were hired not just because they could run a hardware store, but because they were exceptionally good with people. Their strengths and their commitment to building relationships, seeing people, hearing people, and creating teams with purpose and vision are why they were such an invaluable part of this team. He thanked them again for their time and their commitment and reminded them that he'd be on vacation for a week but that he was just a phone call away if they needed him.

"Run your store like you own it!" is how Alex closed out every meeting.

Everybody filed out of the room and to the bar across the street for lunch and drinks. Alex usually joined for the fun, but today he had to run to grab his family and catch his flight. He stood in the doorway and said goodbye to each manager as they left. When Yumiko came up to him, he motioned for her to step aside with him.

"Are you excited to start wedding planning?" Alex asked. The small Asian woman smiled and pulled out her phone. She scrolled through pictures of the wedding venues, and Alex refrained from commenting on the gorgeous land-scaping of the outdoor venue.

"I wanted to let you know that we want to take care of your honeymoon. Wherever you want to go, we will take care of it. If you need to use the jet to get there, we can make it happen.

Yumiko put her hand up to protest, never one to take anything from anyone. But Alex stopped her.

"No, no. Don't even try it. Christy and I are so excited for you and Aiguo; it's been a long time coming, eh? It would be our pleasure. Just let us know what you need," Alex said, smiling from ear to ear, and Yumiko nodded. She knew Alex, and she knew his generosity had no end. She knew if he said he was going to send them on their dream honeymoon, there was no point in resisting.

Alex loved to serve his people; changing lives is what he lived for. He grew up with an absent father, but the way he healed himself was by being incredibly loyal to his people, above and beyond the norm. He did so much for so many people who worked for him, and nobody knew about it most of the time. *Your character is defined by what you do when you don't think anyone's watching*, he would always tell his kids. He didn't care how big or important someone was. He had made more money than he had ever hoped for and loved to share it with his people. Alex didn't need anyone to know how he helped or served his people. He did it because it felt right.

When the room was empty, Alex threw all of the plates and empty containers into the trash. Alex wiped down the table with a paper towel, turned off the lights, and shut the door just as Tamara was pushing her cleaning cart toward him. She looked at the conference room, and it was spotless. She was thankful but not surprised, because Alex did this every time.

No job was too small for Alex. He built this business from the ground up, and he was still the same guy today as he was 20 years ago.

"I was going to clean for you!" she said, in her strong Caribbean accent, pointing to the spotless conference room.

"Oh, no worries, Tamara, I got it. Wasn't that much. That group doesn't make a mess. Thank you, though. The rest of this place looks awesome," he said, gesturing around the office. "How's school?"

"Good! I study hard and stay up late. Almost done with my classes. Two months," she said proudly. Alex smiled and put his hand on her shoulder. "I'm proud of you. But you should be proud of yourself." She beamed, and they said their goodbyes. He settled back into the driver's seat, started his Vacation Mode playlist, and headed home.

Reflection
Alex made it a top priority to connect with his team and infuse a family-oriented atmosphere, ultimately creating a culture built on a foundation of trust. Spend five minutes brainstorming how you can better connect with your people.

2

ABOVE THE HOLE

When Alex walked through the front door, he could feel the excitement. There was a row of matching luggage lined up at the front door, and he could hear 70s pop music blasting from the kitchen. This was a good sign. When Christy was channeling her inner teenager, it meant she was feeling happy, excited, productive, and focused. He hugged her from behind and gave her a quick kiss as she dried the last dish and put it away, never missing a beat from her favorite pop song. Alex was just as invested and alert at home with his home people as he was with his work people.

"What can I do to help?" he asked Christy (the CEO of the home) as he moved out of her way.

"Maybe check on how the boys are doing in the van? And clear out the refrigerator so our food doesn't go bad when we're gone? I'm almost done in the kitchen," Christy said, drying her hands on her apron.

He loved the way she looked when she was excited about something. It was the same way she looked when they went to prom together in high school and when he surprised her with a romantic proposal a few years later. And when she graduated from college, got her dream job, and saw two blue lines on that pregnancy test. And now, as she prepared her family for a well-deserved trip to sunny Florida. He made a mental note to tell her how beautiful she looked when she was happy.

Alex followed the sound of bickering to the driveway, where he found his twins, Max and Milo, arguing over who was supposed to be cleaning which side of the Lincoln Navigator.

"Guys. It will get done a lot faster if you work—"

"Together," they moaned in unison.

Teamwork was always something Alex valued. As part of a big family growing up, his parents relied on him and his siblings to work together to get things done, even more so when his dad left and the kids had to help his mom pick up the pieces.

To this day, he never understood why his dad just bolted. He really just disappeared. No explanation, no warning signs—he just left abruptly and disappeared into the night. The abandonment caused long-term trust issues and anger that he had to learn to manage. Alex, being the youngest, didn't remember much, but his dad did introduce him to golf, so Alex has fonder memories of him than his older siblings.

For years they tried to find him and came up with all types of theories on why his dad left, but their mom kept it together. Alex's mom could always brighten up a room; even as a single mom she never lost her smile or her love for people. Her family needed her to stay strong and step up, and she kept them focused on the future and didn't let them dwell in anger or resentment. Alex would hear her cry at night, and he would go in and just hug his momma. She thought Alex gave the best hugs. He never forgot the feeling and wished he could have done more for his mom.

Alex learned how to love people by his mom's example. As he became a father, the idea of leaving his family made him sick to his stomach. He couldn't fathom how anyone could live with themselves after that. But he used the pain and trauma to be the best dad he could be for his kids and the best business leader possible. He was determined to break the cycle and always be there for everyone.

After checking on the boys, Alex walked around the yard. Alex was meticulous with their landscaping. They had the nicest yard in the neighborhood, not one shrub was out of place, and not one blade of grass was malnourished. His neighbors never understood why such a successful man wouldn't pay a landscaping company to do it for him. As Alex did the yard, he would think and work out all the problems of the world in his own head. Nobody bothered him as he did his yard work. Tree Boy would go into a zone. Alex designed the landscaping and planted each and every tree, shrub, and flower. He would check the yard every day before he went to work and a second time when he got home. Alex was obsessive about his landscape.

When times were tight after his dad left, Alex picked up hours and worked at the local golf courses so he could keep golfing and fulfill his dream of being a pro golfer one day, an idea Alex's dad put in his head. He loved his daddy and fondly remembers the day his dad introduced him to golf.

Golf is a high-end sport, so it was expensive to pay for the green fees and have access to the driving range at the challenging courses. Working at the course allowed him to make a little money to take care of himself, and he could play the course for free. The best days were when he caddied as the tips made him feel like he was rich. He became a star employee at the golf course where he worked all throughout school.

As a suburban teen and young adult, he tried to hide the fact that he worked at a golf course from his friends as he didn't want anyone to look down on him or feel sorry for him. All of his other golfer friends lived in fancy houses and gated communities and were active at the local country clubs. Their parents could afford the addiction to this expensive sport, and every so often he heard the way their parents talked about the staff, the janitors, the groundskeeping team, and even the beverage cart drivers. He didn't want his friends, or his friends' parents, thinking of him like that.

But Alex had no idea how much teamwork was needed to run a golf course; he never noticed or paid attention. He quickly learned what went into running a top golf course behind the scenes. It was a world he never thought of as a golfer. The staff was always the backdrop as he focused on lowering his handicap and making sure he could compete and win at every tournament against his peer group.

Over time, Alex did everything you could think of at the golf course. He was always the first to volunteer for a task or step up and help someone who needed it. He didn't care if it wasn't in his job description or not in his department. He just wanted to stay busy. He wanted to help people. He wanted to be part of something good. They had HR resources, a marketing team, catering teams, and several staff who ran each restaurant and bar on property, and Alex dabbled in all of it. It was like he got to peek backstage and stumbled into Oz. A new world within a world. He had seen many golf courses and country clubs, but now he was seeing them in a whole new light. These valets, servers, and beverage cart people had names.

The landscaping crews were the most amazing of all the teams. They got the courses looking pristine and had to keep them pristine at all times. He never noticed the huge warehouse tucked away within the courses that housed all the equipment. His favorite country club job had a crew that had to manage two different championship courses. The members demanded excellence and always talked about what shape the course was in!

The nicer the course, the larger the crew. He often wondered if he didn't make it as a pro golfer, maybe he could design courses. When Alex was excused to go and play in weekend tournaments, his skin would crawl when his bratty friends would criticize a course, but they rarely bragged about its beauty. *Those greens are too fast; the range has way too many divots. Where are the racks for the sand trap?* The expectation was perfection, and that made the landscaper's job that much more difficult.

Alex received a college scholarship to play golf but worked at the courses in college to make sure he always had some money in his pocket. He loved it too.

The best part about spending so much time working behind the scenes at the top golf courses in town was that it is where he met Christy. Her dad, James Gray, was a well-known player at the golf course and would come frequently with business partners and other well-known people in the community. One sunny Saturday, Mr. Gray came in, and Alex rushed over to offer his assistance. Mr. Gray complimented Alex on his hustle and hard work and said he saw a lot of himself in Alex's work ethic. The conversation was interrupted when another man in an expensive suit walked up to Mr. Gray and asked him to step aside for a serious conversation. Before he stepped aside, Mr. Gray asked Alex if he would walk Christy through the grounds and show her around while he handled some business. This was a high-end men's-only golf club where businesspeople wheeled and dealed.

The two spent close to an hour walking and talking and connected immediately, and as their time together ended,

Alex took a deep breath and asked for her number. He was speechless when Christy scribbled her number on a piece of paper and handed it to him. He called her that night, and the rest was history.

Together, Alex and Christy had a whirlwind romance, got married right out of college, and lived in a tiny apartment in a questionable part of town. Her father offered to loan them money to move closer to the city (and to them), but Alex politely declined.

He was skeptical of Christy's dad and wondered if his father-in-law would feel like he owned him if he took money from him. Alex and Christy lived modestly, said no to a lot of things they really wanted to do but couldn't afford, and worked multiple odd jobs to save. Christy could have made one call to her dad to easily handle all of their financial hardships, but she respected Alex for what he had been through and what he was becoming. She trusted his work ethic, and so did her dad. Weirdly, he trusted Alex way more because he didn't want any handouts. Mr. Gray saw himself in Alex, and that gave him instant peace even though Alex was a little standoffish with Mr. Gray. He didn't want to let another dad hurt him. Later as they bonded, Mr. Gary confessed to Alex that he would have been the only employee he would have asked to show his daughter around.

Alex was also thankful that Christy took over the role of the financial manager and kept a close eye on their accounts.

It took only a few bounced checks for them to realize that his math wasn't always reliable and that it would be better for them (and their bank account) for her to handle the numbers. He had a quick-ending pro golf career and never secured his tour card consistently, but they saved every dime they made in his fledgling career. It was important to Alex that Christy was involved in their financial goals. He needed Christy involved in the day-to-day and to be his true partner in everything, especially the money part.

They were a good team, and when they finally decided they were as ready as they'd ever be to start a family, they also realized it wasn't going to be as easy as it was for their newly pregnant friends. They were patient, but negative test after negative test took a toll on them and their marriage. Christy wanted to be a mom and felt like a failure every time the test came up negative. Alex was disappointed but didn't know how to comfort her.

Finally, after countless doctor's appointments, late-night fights, and a total change in their diet, Alex woke up when he heard Christy screech from their tiny bathroom. The test was positive, and they cried and held each other on the bathroom floor.

Austin was born 34 weeks later, and they figured out the parenting thing as a team. It took five years for them to get pregnant again, but Ollie made his appearance swiftly and quickly in an unplanned home birth, and thanks to IVF, the twins came three years later.

Raising kids and working full time wasn't easy for Alex. As Red's Hardware grew, he began to travel. Short drives eventually gave way to short flights, but they relied on their foundation of teamwork and communication and fell into a rhythm. Alex loved the art and science of teamwork. His large family coming together as a team after his dad left and working at the golf course made Alex realize that the best part of life is teamwork.

Alex was the ultimate family guy. He saw his world as his family-people and his work-people. He devoted all of his time to both. However, there was one exception. Alex was intentional about his yearly golf trip to stay connected with his college golf teammates. It was the one thing he fought for and insisted he attend every year. He normally traveled alone, but Christy and the entire family were making the trek this time to meet Bobbi and Collin.

On this trip, there was another element of the vacation that Alex was looking forward to. He was going to spend some quality time with his oldest daughter in the form of a round of golf with his college friends. He couldn't believe she was about to graduate high school, and it made him feel extra ancient that she would be taking some of the same classes he did 20 years earlier, in the same buildings, at the same university. He invited her to join him for a day on the course with his college friends.

Golf was a hobby they both loved. Austin could have played in college herself but opted to completely focus on school; it was a decision that, although painful for Alex, he completely agreed with. He respected Austin for her mature decision. This trip was a chance to reconnect with his buddies but also help prepare Austin for the new chapter of her life. Cultivate: Secret Business Fundamentals for Business Leaders was on her schedule for the fall, and it was a low-key introductory business class that Alex felt had shaped his entire business career.

Alex still had his notes from that class and reviewed them often. He always dreamed of handing them over to Austin like they were the Dead Sea scrolls. A few weeks earlier, Alex had reached out to Bobbi and asked her to help him with a special project. He wanted to save all of these notes electronically and make it easy for Austin to save, use, and access them. Bobbi managed to scan all of Alex's handwritten notes and create a QR code. Alex's fatherly dream was that if Austin scanned the code and had all of the notes on her phone, she'd review them regularly, and they'd help her as much as they helped him. When he told his idea to Christy, she smiled at him sweetly. It was a smile that meant "Oh, honey, that's a very sweet thought but. . .college is over. Let it go, dude." Christy was such a feisty straight shooter but she loved her Tree Boy and never went in too deep with her sweetheart.

He had reached out to friends Bobbi and Collin a few months before making their final plans for their day on the green. He called and texted obsessively to finalize the details, and Bobbi and Collin never understood how such a successful business guy with more than 150 locations had so much time to focus on planning a golf trip, spend time with his large family, *and* enjoy life. They were both business leaders in their own right, but they could barely find time to sleep! And they always were overwhelmed and exhausted. Bobbi recommended the location this time, and Alex followed through.

In college, his GPA was nowhere near theirs (which they reminded him of regularly), he didn't have the same family background or support, and he struggled in all the business courses like Economics, Business Theory, and especially Accounting. Bobbi and Collin aced all three. They didn't completely get how Alex did it. How did this guy have the biggest, most successful business, yet he didn't have the background or the books smarts they did.

They all loved golf and business, but other than that, the trio came from completely different worlds. Bobbi and Collin were stud golfers, and Alex got recruited because of his work ethic and attitude and raving reviews from the golf coach and golf pros in the area. He was not a naturally gifted golfer, but he made up with grit, attitude, and determination. He worked tirelessly on his golf game, chipping and putting for hours upon hours. He willed himself into a scholarship.

Alex didn't have many fond memories of spending one-on-one time with his dad, so he was honored that Austin was as excited about the golf game as he was. Alex wanted to make sure he could connect Austin with Bobbi because being a female in business is different, and Alex respected that. He hoped that Bobbi and Austin hit it off and that Bobbi would become Austin's mentor.

When they got to the airport, Alex followed the signs for the private hangars. He parked and saw that Jimmy was already doing the preflight inspection on the Gulfstream G100. Alex still couldn't believe that he had a private jet, but it made doing business so much easier and allowed him to get to and from his stores across the country much easier. His kids had a hard time with the private jet, as they thought it was too flashy. Their reaction to it made Alex proud. He was intentional about raising humble, grateful, appreciative kids that the fact that they wanted to take a commercial airline instead meant he was doing something right. He vividly remembers some of the annoying entitled kids from the country clubs where he worked and vowed not to raise some himself. When he wasn't using the jet, Alex always made sure to donate flight time to local charities that meant something to him and his family. He hated the thought of his jet just sitting in the hangar when it could be used to help other people.

It had taken him a long time to get used to the fact that he had made it to a point in his life where a private jet made sense. His kids were still getting there. Christy, on the other hand, was all about it. She loved that it took the stress out of their travels, that it meant fewer luggage restrictions, and that it made it easier for Alex to check in on his stores that were far away. He could jump on the plane to hang the sign in a new store, solve problems, and host important meetings without his kids even noticing he was gone. When they were little, he would see them either in the morning before school or at dinner, but he rarely missed both. Whenever he felt uncomfortable or awkward about the jet, Christy would remind him that it was a business decision that allowed him to spend more time with his family and his work people. She always knew that bringing up *people*, specifically spending time with people, would help ease his anxiety.

"We're almost set, boss," Jimmy said with a smile. He had been Alex's pilot for a long time, and Alex trusted him with his life. Literally. Jasmine, the flight attendant, offered refreshments and to take all of their backpacks, but Ollie, Max, and Milo instinctively stepped in. The three of them were able to get all their backpacks, plus Alex's, Christie's, and Austin's, and put them away just like dad taught them. Christie talked with Jasmine about how her kids were and what she was planning to do with her upcoming time off.

When they hired their flight crew, Alex wanted to make sure that he actually got to know them. He hated getting on private jets with other business owners who barely even acknowledged the people who were flying the plane or helping them throughout the flight. Alex and his family felt like they knew Jimmy and Jasmine personally and often invited them to holiday parties.

Everyone settled into their seats. Max and Milo were already trying to figure out the Wi-Fi, Austin was already lost in her book, and Ollie was looking out the window. Alex winked at Christy, and she gave him a big smile to let him know that she was proud of him.

"Is dad crying yet?" one of the boys called from behind him. Alex laughed and quickly wiped a tear. He couldn't help it. The private jet always reminded him of how hard he had worked and how far he had come. He was so thankful that all of his success hasn't changed him at his core and that all of his work toward not raising entitled, bratty kids seemed to be working.

"Stop it, Milo," Christy ordered, squeezing Alex's hand again, "Your dad is in touch with his emotions, and I love that about him. Vulnerability is hot," she said, winking at him. She knew that would shut her boys up, and it did. Christy was quick to defend her man, and Alex worked hard to make sure he was worthy.

He held her hand and squeezed, a simple gesture to remind her that he was right there. He wasn't going anywhere, and he would never leave no matter how much pressure they faced. He was not his father. Christy returned the squeeze, and her body relaxed. She felt safe and protected and provided for. She was right where she wanted to be. Alex and Christy both had the dream life they had always wanted.

Reflection

Alex was keenly aware that he wasn't the best student or golfer naturally, yet he went on to be the most successful of his group of friends because of his grit, attitude, and determination throughout school and into his business-building years. Not being "the best" doesn't dictate how successful you will be in that area; it indicates the areas to dig in and add grit and determination to that area of your life. Identify two to three areas in your life that could use some more grit to help you create the life you've dreamed of.

3

SHORT-SIDED

B obbi walked into her spacious master closet and surveyed her options. Designer clothes hung from metal racks, separated and organized by color, season, and style. Summer dresses here, business jackets over there, and an entire wall devoted completely to shoes. Her favorite feature of the closet was the center island, a convenient space to fold clothes that also had drawers for her intimates, accessories, pajamas, and favorite rock band T-shirts. One corner of the closet was dedicated to golf attire, so she shifted her focus there. She carefully flipped through the polo shirts and pleated pants, dresses, hats, and purses until she found just the right combination. After a long shower and the completion of her meticulous hair, skin, and makeup routine, Bobbi checked the full-length mirror beside the French doors that led out to her balcony. Bobbi was always stylin' and profilin'—always dressed to the nines. Bobbi credited many of her stylish outfits to D'Shawn, her personal stylist who often did the shopping for her when Bobbi didn't have the time. This was the life Bobbi was used to.

She put her hands on her hips and stared at her reflection. Her commitment to a rigorous workout routine and her husband's unmatched ability to create healthy gourmet meals showed in her tight and muscular physique. She liked the way the pink polo popped against her dark skin, and she felt like a boss. She hustled down the spiral staircase into the gleaming kitchen, where Dale was pouring her green smoothie into a to-go cup. He was shirtless and making her food, and she wondered if she needed to leave the house at all. He smiled at her and handed her the cup and her insulated lunch bag, packed with glass containers of sous vide duck, cilantro rice, and veggies sauteed perfectly in extra virgin olive, imported from Italy.

"Have a great trip, babe. I'll hold down the fort. Jordan has a soccer game tonight and her. . ."

"Don't forget to wash her blue jersey," Bobbi interrupted, pointing to the laundry room.

"Blue jersey is already washed," Dale finished.

"It's our week to do snacks and juices, so I made fruit cups and mini sandwiches. I made sure. . ." Dale started again.

"The Ramsey twins can't have gluten!" she said in a panic, heading for the fridge.

"And I made sure to do four gluten-free options for the Ramsey twins," he finished again, playfully blocking the refrigerator. "I can do this, you know. I've been doing it for years," he said, giving Bobbi a reassuring look.

"We'll do church in the morning, and then the Dad Squad is meeting at Lakeside Park after," he said, looking at the calendar on the fridge. She smiled. She loved that he had the Dad Squad. It was a group of five to eight other stay-at-home dads who met up a few times a week with their kids at playgrounds, splash pads, or pool days at their respective houses. It started out as an oddly new thing for Dale, but he was getting the hang of it. Dale was secure enough in himself and willing to make it work. Bobbi was known to be a little vain and loved attention, but Dale didn't lack confidence either. They made it work, all of it. And Bobbi loved and appreciated the sacrifice that Dale made for their relationship to work.

Bobbi wasn't ashamed of the fact she loved business, she loved her industry, and she was committed to success and growth. She used to feel guilty about not wanting to sacrifice herself for a family and would avoid questions from her mom and sisters about when she was going to settle down and have a family. Bobbi dreamed of being a successful businessperson just like her dad, a retired executive from IBM, while her sisters focused on being just like their mom, a retired IBM sales rep who hit the jackpot when she married her dad. As soon as they tied the knot, mom retired and gave up her career for the family.

She didn't want to settle down. And she wasn't against a family; she just didn't want to have to choose. When she met Dale, he was an executive chef and owner at one of the most popular restaurants in downtown Sacramento. Dale made tons of money for years but got burned out from the stress of running a Michelin Star restaurant. All of his plaques were packed away in the garage. Dale wasn't afraid of Bobbi's drive because he understood it.

He wasn't scared of her passion, and her success didn't make him feel inferior.

His dad was from Mozambique, and his mom was a white South African woman; and they produced the most handsome son Bobbi had ever seen. Beautiful caramel skin, green eyes, and the body of a great athlete. He had the means to take care of both of them for life, but was very secure with her working outside the home instead. The chemistry was amazing, and the attraction was pure. Dale was blown away by Bobbi's chocolate beauty, but her confidence is what captured his heart. Bobbi knew how to handle herself around confident men, and that closed the deal for Dale.

As a Black woman in a mostly male-dominated industry, Bobbi knew that meeting a man like Dale was rare. Bobbi always chose male-dominated industries and was always ready for the challenge. One of the biggest issues she faced was pertaining to the double standard that came with being emotional in the workplace. When a male business leader was firm and clear about his expectations, he was authoritative, powerful, decisive. But when Bobbi did or said the same things, she was called many colorful names. On the rare occasion when one of her male colleagues teared up or got emotional during a meeting, he was praised for being highly invested and passionate. But of course the *one* time Bobbi got emotional and shed a few tears during a highly emotional meeting, there were whispers that she was too emotional, too hormonal, and maybe not strong enough to handle the stress and lead. She was used to the double standard, which made Dale's confidence in her a breath of fresh air.

When things got serious between Dale and Bobbi, she wanted to move to Nashville to launch GolfTek. Dale surprised his investors by cashing out and doing what needed to be done so he could follow her to Nashville. He picked up a few private chef gigs here and there, but for the most part, he was happy being whatever she needed him to be. The grocery store runner, the kid-taxi, the house manager, the ultimate scheduler, the cleaner, the chef, the attentive dad, and the dreamy husband: he did it all at home so she could do it all at the office. And he had an uncanny ability to do it all while she relentlessly attempted to micromanage everything.

Bobbi would try her best to micromanage the house too, but Dale wouldn't let her. The constant micromanaging concerned him a bit, because micromanaging is what burned him out. He has been delivered from the micromanage movement and was praying for his wife to be delivered too. He had his hand on everything at the restaurant until he was on the verge of a nervous breakdown, so he understood the micromanager and the dangers as well. Part of what made their relationship work was that Dale saw himself in Bobbi. The good, the bad, and the beautiful.

The pressure of performing as a top chef for one restaurant was stressful as his investors hounded him to open another. He hit rock bottom when he was out one night with a few chefs drinking and was offered a little white baggy to help him take the edge off. He was desperate, and they sold him on cocaine as the answer to the stress of being a top chef. They were offering an escape from the constant pressure and stress that came with the demand of late nights and the constant pressure from food critics. In the industry, cocaine was easy to find, and Dale found himself relying on it to get the job done. When Bobbi found evidence of a white substance on the counter in the bathroom, she knew it wasn't flour. She called him out on it. Drugs were a deal-breaker for her, and he had to make a choice. Neither of them felt his habit required rehab, and both were confident that stress was the trigger for him. So Dale knew he had to pivot or who knows what would happen.

The move to Nashville was a fresh start for both of them. In Nashville, Dale was not a celebrity chef constantly under pressure. He was a nobody in Nashville, unimportant and he loved it. They both settled into their roles: her as the busy bread winner and him as the manager of the house. Dale was good at letting her lead in her role, but Bobbi struggled to grow her business through the years and was frustrated. Strong-willed and stubborn, change doesn't come easy for Bobbi.

She parked her Range Rover in her designated spot and walked quickly into the office. The sliding glass doors separated as she approached, and she walked into the modern front lobby. She loved the way the large windows filled the space with natural light and how the open design of the office allowed one space to flow into the next, perfect for collaboration. *Industrial chic* is the feeling she was going for when she gave the OK for the office renovation, complete with hardwood floors, exposed metal beams, and islands of work desks with sleek laptops and rolling chairs. Gorgeous landscape pictures of famous golf courses lined the walls, and a single-hole putting green in the back corner of the building added a pop of color to the space.

Bobbi designed the decor and picked out everything from the tile on the floor to every light fixture. Bobbi didn't need an interior designer because she trusted her eye more than others. The only reason she has D'Shawn is because she is just too busy to shop herself. Bobbi was a bad chick ,and she let you know it.

She was proud of what she built. A Black woman-owned tech company wasn't unheard of in Nashville, but it sure wasn't the norm. Bobbi was used to being the exception to the norm. She was the only Black woman on her college golf team and one of the few Black women in her business classes. She was the female star golfer on the team, and her love of golf and technology launched her into creating GolfTek, an innovative tech company "geared toward enhancing the golf experience." In an industry dominated by men, Bobbi enjoyed the rush that came with pushing the boundaries and exceeding expectations.

Her company created software that allowed golfers to have a mini-golf coach in their pocket, programmed right into their smartphone. GolfTek technology helped golfers improve their swing, allowed them to use GPS to track their golf balls, and partnered with some of the best golf courses in the country to create a customized experience for users. No need for a caddie to suggest a club or to help; you read the green. GolfTek was right there with you for every stroke. All of her clients loved her, and she was often sighted in business magazines as a business wiz; publications targeted to women and African Americans chased her down for interviews, and she looked perfect on the cover of a magazine.

It was because of her business connections that Bobbi was able to snag a tee time at one of the most famous resorts in Florida. The Breakers of Palm Beach is one of the most exclusive golf courses in the country, and she was excited to finally get out on the green and play a round. She had been to the impressive resort many times for executive-level meetings and conferences, but she had never been there on vacation to just enjoy it. All of the successful businesspeople with old money know about the Breakers, and Bobbi felt right at home. Bobbi always felt like if you have not heard of The Breakers, you weren't their target customer. It's the ultimate "if you know, you know" type of resort. Her dad had been a few times through the years and loved the place too.

Bobbi walked over to the team of techies in the center of the room, looking intently at their screens. "Don't forget to CC me on that," Bobbi said, pointing to Carmen's screen. She wasn't sure who the email was to or what it was about, but Bobbi wanted to know. She wanted to be involved in all aspects of business and hated when people made decisions big or small without her approval.

"Are you going to keep that like that. . .?" she asked TJ, pointing at the bottom-right corner of his screen.

"I'm still editing. It's not done yet. It won't be like that when it's finished," he said, sounding slightly annoyed. She made her way to each person, standing over them and analyzing their screens from behind.

"Can I get an update on that?" she asked Paul.

"Don't forget to send me a detailed report on your progress," she reminded Lamar.

"You're still on this part?" she asked Stacy, trying not to sound disappointed.

Now she was again wondering if she should leave town, but for another reason. Being away meant not being able to oversee the day-to-day activities of the office. It meant leaving each project up to the team and risking not being involved in big decisions. Or small decisions. Bobbi had been through so many COOs everyone had lost count, including Bobbi.

She knew she needed a COO, but nobody was good enough, despite national searches and high recommendations. The control freak in her would make them angry within the first few months or she wouldn't like their ideas or changes. Bobbi was more interested in controlling, but she thought it was leading.

"Do you have that QR code emailed over to me yet?" she asked Craig.

"Yep. Sent it to you at. . .," he checked his phone, "1:04 a.m. Right after you called and asked me about it. And the binder with your friend's college notes is on your desk," Craig said flatly.

Bobbi smiled approvingly. "Bobbi, can we talk about my salary? A raise?" Craig asked, following quickly behind Bobbi as she moved through the space. "It's been a few years now, and I need. . .and I hit my bonus each year I have been here until you moved the goal post!" Craig called from behind her. Bobbi stopped when she noticed people were watching and turned to face Craig.

She quietly dismissed the conversation and said, "When I get back from vacation, we can talk about it."

For some reason Bobbi didn't like the bonus concept and secretly rooted for her people to not achieve their bonuses. *I need to keep expenses down*, she thought. Meanwhile she spared no expense on her lifestyle.

She stood at the front of the room and cleared her throat. Her team turned in their rolling chairs to face her. Bobbi could own a room naturally but also demanded attention. She was cute and very personable, but she wore on people over time.

"Hey, everyone. Happy to see you. I'm going out of town for a few days, but it's still business as usual. Send me everything you're working on by the end of the day for my review, and I'll get back to you with edits or suggestions. Or I'll do it myself and send you an email, depending on what it is. Please make sure you're keeping a detailed log of your daily tasks too. I'll be back on Tuesday; we'll have a meeting to discuss everything that was done while I was away. Call or text me if anything comes up; I'll always have this with me," she said, holding up her iPhone.

She stepped into her office, checked her emails, and debated setting up an "Out of Office" message. She knew herself, and she knew she didn't want anyone to think she was taking a break. Perception was everything for Bobbi. She'd be glued to her phone most of the trip and would respond to whatever work emails came through as usual. She grabbed Alex's notebook, shut off the lights, and walked back through the lobby, trying not to look too obvious as she analyzed the computer screens one more time as she walked by.

Something caught her eye on Chris' computer, and she stopped. "Oh, hey, Chris, I can do that. Send it to me; I'll finish it."

"Bobbi, I got it. Don't worry about it, I can handle. . ."

"Oh, I know, but I'll just. . .let me just put the finishing touches on the proposal. I've got a knack. . .." She reached over his shoulder and, with two clicks, sent his project through cyberspace and into her inbox. She didn't look back to see his shocked expression and didn't know that as soon as she was through the front door and in her car, he was packing up his space and heading home. For good, and holding up a one-finger salute on his way to the car. His colleagues didn't even try to stop him, because they understood. If it weren't for their mortgages, car notes, and college tuition—not to mention fear!—they'd be gone too. For many, Bobbi was much too much, and working for her took a toll on her team.

Her team felt that it was impossible to express themselves through their work, and she was so hands-on they rarely got credit for doing anything. Turnover was high, and morale was low. Bobbi recruited confident high achievers like herself—type A personalities—but she micromanaged many right out of the door. And she always justified it or blamed the employee. Bobbi was known for saying things like, "Young people aren't committed like me." or "It's hard to find good help" or "I'm a no-nonsense straight shooter and people don't like that" or "My level of excellence is tough on people so I understand why they leave."

When she wasn't around, her team had a few not so nice ways to describe Bobbi. Clueless was one of them. It was so clear to everyone else that Bobbi was not aware of herself and how she impacted the people around her and the culture of her company. Bobbi worked so hard to fit in and excel, but she lacked self-awareness and couldn't lead others well. This was mostly because her whole day was consumed with Bobbi and her drive to win big. Golf was the perfect sport for her; she got to control her own results and her own outcomes. She hated team sports, and she didn't know how to be co-dependent or trust other people, something Dale knew but still loved her despite this flaw.

At the airport, Bobbi got her custom golf bag out of the truck and watched the valet driver speed away in her SUV with the personalized plate "Chozn 1." She knew this airport well and could navigate the sprawling building while mindlessly scrolling on her phone. She moved her way through security and double-checked that her flight was on time before heading to the exclusive member's area by the gate. She ordered a cocktail at the empty bar and sat back in the luxury lounge furniture overlooking the runway. She checked her emails and then opened up an app that allowed her to see what was going on across the different screens in the office. It's not spying, she reminded herself, "because it's in their contract that their work and use of technology could be monitored and recorded."

She sipped her gin and tonic and scrolled through the busy screens, carefully watching how each of her employees was working. She opened another app to check the security footage for the office and watch the black-and-white footage of her techs walking from one office to another, collaborating around expensive equipment, and working diligently on their screens.

She put her phone down and leaned back on the comfortable furniture. She was excited to see Alex and Collin and finally meet Alex's daughter, Austin. She hoped she could connect with Austin and encourage her to be a fearless and powerful businesswoman. She knew the obstacles that women faced in business and wanted to give Austin advice that would help her through those adversities. She was also excited for the guys to try out GolfTek on the green and show them the innovative features it could add to their golf games. She was proud of the company that she built and wanted to share it with people who knew her from the beginning. Growth was stagnant, but GolfTek still was a sexy thing that could disrupt the golf industry.

She ordered another gin and tonic and texted Dale. She reminded him to let Porky, their 8-pound Chihuahua mix, out each day. He responded with an eye roll emoji and sarcastically thanked her for reminding him. "Glad you reminded me," he texted back. And instead of saying "Honey, I have run top restaurants all over the world; I have served 200 tables on a slow night with a staff of 50 people, valet, and a crowded kitchen. I can surely run one house, with one dog and one child," he replied with,

"I would have completely forgotten to let our dog out for three days if you weren't in my life," followed by another eye roll, a wink, and a dog emoji.

When it was time for boarding, Bobbi headed to the gate. When they called for first-class boarding, Bobbi rolled her suitcase to the terminal entrance, down the gangway, and to her window seat and ignored the eye rolls as she pushed her way to her seat. She flew first class every time or she wouldn't go. Bobbi was always dreaming of the day that she would have her own plane with the streamlined GolfTek logo right on the side. She has a folder saved to her desktop with pictures and specs for the plane that she wants once her business takes off. She already has design ideas of how she wants to decorate it.

She opened up her laptop and was slightly annoyed as she waited for the plane's Wi-Fi to engage. She checked emails again, logged into the GolfTek website to work on administrative duties, and gave in to the temptation to check the security cameras one more time. "Oh shoot, I almost forgot the payroll!" Bobbi said aloud. Bobbi frantically called in payroll and just made the cutoff to get her people paid. Yes, she still calls in payroll; her HR department is small, and they are the most frustrated members of the team. Before she knew it, the wheels were up, they were headed to sunny Florida, and instantly the Energizer Bunny fell asleep.

Reflection
Bobbi is highly ambitious and driven to succeed in business. Her drive and ambition makes her blind to her micromanaging tendencies and the lack of trust and camaraderie it creates on her team. Reflect on your day-to-day interactions with your family and team. Do you constantly check on every detail that somebody else is supposed to take care of? Do you often take over others' work midstream?

4

Chip Shot

Collin woke up startled by the beeping of his alarm. It took a second to register where he was, until he looked to his right to see Jada, still sleeping. Then the memories of the night before came flooding back, along with the initial symptoms of a hangover. He got out of bed, careful not to disturb her, and walked into the hotel bathroom. He closed the door, started the shower, and looked at himself in the mirror. He needed to shave, and he needed a haircut, but that would have to wait. He needed to get home and pack. He stepped into the steaming shower and let the water run over him. When he stepped out, Jada was sitting up in bed, with a thin hotel sheet pulled over her, and greeted him with a knowing smile.

He leaned over the bed, kissed her, and then looked around the room for his clothes. His pants were in a jumbled pile on the floor, and his shoes were by the front door. He got dressed, trying to avoid Jada's sad stare. If he allowed himself to look at her, he'd get lost in those seductive brown eyes and never make his flight.

"I have to go," he said, scanning the room to make sure he didn't leave anything behind. She pouted. He resisted.

"I'll only be gone a few days. It'll be fine. I'll call you when I can," he assured her. She sighed, and he winked as he closed the hotel room behind him. He checked his phone, got into his car, and drove home.

When he arrived home, he was relieved that he was the only one there. Amy had gone out of town to visit her sister for a few days and was due back later that morning. Collin parked in the garage, threw his clothes into the washer, and went upstairs to change. He pulled a suitcase out of the closet and threw in a few essentials. He grabbed his Titleist golf bag from the walk-in closet and swung it over his shoulder. And he made sure he grabbed both of his cell phones.

He was excited about this golf trip and relieved his night out went undetected. Being on the green was one of his favorite places to be. He grew up a loner around the perfectly landscaped golf courses in Sag Harbor and loved the atmosphere of the exclusive golf clubs his parents were members of. As a young kid, he took golf lessons and went to golf camp every summer. It was his natural ability on the green that got him a spot on the college golf team. He loved golf because he didn't have to rely on or trust anyone. Collin would always bet on himself and was used to getting whatever or whomever he wanted. Collin was handsome, athletic, and very sure of himself.

He could have gone to school anywhere in the country. His high-profile parents had the means and desire to send him to any prestigious school and were delighted when he was accepted to their alma mater in Florida. It was a bit of an adjustment, playing on a college team. Golf is an individual sport, and he was used to the attention he got from being the star player on his high school team and playing in tournaments around the country as an amateur. He expected a little more competition at the college level, but Collin is what people would call a stud. He was as gifted a golfer as you could find, and his parents invested heavily in his development. He had a swing coach, a personal trainer, a nutritionist, and a mental coach all in high school, and he soon grew bored of the lack of competition in his age group. All he would watch on TV was the golf channel, and he locked onto the pro golf community and didn't pay much attention to his own community. His parents had to beg him to work hard and stay focused, but his raw talent was undeniable. *Either people have it or they don't.* He had a few swing coaches during high school career that were fired when they challenged Collin to work harder and not rely on his talent alone.

He was used to having things go his way and felt like any form of critique or feedback was an attack. His mindset was always, *The way I play golf, I will make it all on my own. I don't need anyone.* He saw it as the "golfer's personality" and felt all great golfers were wired this way.

His support system and the facilities he had access to in high school were so good that going to college was a step down for him. His coach tried to remind him that his teammates weren't his competition and that everyone was working together toward the same goal. But Collin had never been exposed to the team concept in his life, and he was the best golfer the moment he walked onto campus.

He was a brilliant student; all of his grades and test scores were off the charts, and he rarely studied. He had it all.

Being the best was who he was. It was what was expected. And he had zero time or patience for people who didn't measure up. He wondered many times why his golf coach spent so much time teaching other members of the team the intricacies and skills required to play the game. If they got this far and still struggled with a chip shot from a thick rough to a downward sloping green, they shouldn't be on the team. Plain and simple. *Either you got it or you don't.* He saw mentoring young players as a waste of time. "It's not my job to mentor them; they need to figure it out as I did."

He breezed through law school and passed the bar the first time. He only had to send out three applications before being accepted to work at a prestigious law firm just 15 minutes from his house, the same firm he is now a partner with.

He got back in the car and headed to the office. He wanted to be gone before Amy got home. He was too tired to fight or cover his lies that were starting to pile up.

The Law Offices of Moreland and Myers was a historic brick building in a bustling and affluent city in Bridgehampton. The lobby was bright and airy and featured luxury leather furniture, glass coffee tables piled with a variety of different magazines, and subtle blue and orange finishes, a quiet nod to his alma mater. Clients would wait here to meet with him or another lawyer on his team and then follow a narrow hallway down to a row of spacious and private offices.

Collin's office was down the hallway at the very end, a sprawling corner office with floor-to-ceiling windows that looked out over a lush, green community park. His handcrafted oak desk was meticulously organized, and the built-in shelves behind his rolling computer chair were packed with books about law, ethics, and history.

Pictures of Collin shaking hands with professional golfers lined the walls, and his certifications, awards, and accolades hang on the wall adjacent to the entry door so that it was the first thing that people noticed when they walked in. On the other side of the hallway were a few conference rooms where lawyers could meet with clients in a more open space and where Collin could lead meetings with his team.

Collin loved being a lawyer, but he was still bitter that his pro golf career didn't pan out the way he hoped, and he routinely reminded everyone how it wasn't his fault. He blamed his coaches, his trainers, his agents, his injuries, and as crazy as it sounds. . .his parents. He would easily and frequently blame the same hard-working people who gave him every luxury in life a kid could ask for. His own inadequacies and lack of people skills made everything he did more difficult than it should have been. Nothing was his fault. He had been called "uncoachable" and just walked to his own beat. When he hurt his back, he didn't even follow the rehabilitation prescribed from the doctors.

In college, Collin's golf game didn't get better; it seemed as if he peaked in high school. But the truth was, he just stopped working and improving. Alex and Bobbi both marveled at how good Collin was naturally. They were good, but nobody was as talented as Collin. He thrived in all three phases of golf: his tee shots were powerful, his approach shots were flawless, and he could putt with the best even under pressure. This kid was a can't-miss pro golfer and bell cow of the recruiting class; he had a reason to feel so good about himself.

Shelly, his young, gorgeous, and efficient secretary, had recently taken it upon herself to transform the bleak and boring break room into a modern hang-out space with a coffee shop feel, complete with bright area rugs, coffee-themed decor, decorative floor lamps, high-end furniture, and a complete coffee bar in the corner. It was a welcomed feminine touch in an office dominated by men. Shelly wasn't the most skilled receptionist, but Collin decided to bring her on board, and nobody knew what that was all about either. She worked for the firm, but she paid special attention to Collin and everything he needed. The other lawyers noticed the way she'd run her hand across his back when she walked by or how they'd both happen to take very long lunch breaks at the same time. She was a single mom with two kids and was very vulnerable, and everyone who knew Collin and how opportunistic he could be assumed the worst with those two.

Collin loved the ladies, especially if he was stressed out about something. He had the perfect wife at home; many people who knew him couldn't believe she fell for him. Everyone knew about his shenanigans but couldn't say a word or feel the wrath of Collin. Morale was very low, and Collin didn't have a clue as to why.

Collin could hear quiet murmuring coming from the offices around him. His team was always busy with scheduling, consulting, long-winded phone calls, and client meetings. They were the best personal injury lawyers in the state and worked with many high-profile clients. Collin looked up from his pile of paperwork when he heard a knock at the door. It was Trent Myers, Collin's law partner and childhood best friend.

"Good news and bad news," Trent said, leaning in the doorway. Collin waited.

"Good news is that we have a long list of up-and-coming lawyers who want to fill his spot," Trent started. Collin looked confused.

"So the bad news is. . .?" Collin gestured with his hands for Trent to move the story along.

"The Mendez family fired Scott," Trent said quickly, "citing poor communication and lack of results," Trent said, using air quotes. Collin cracked his knuckles.

"Does he know?" Collin asked, sitting back in his leather chair.

"That we're letting him go? Not yet. Wanted to check with you first."

"Obviously. We don't have time for this. His results with the Rossi family were subpar, and I just think he's too new, and he doesn't have the It factor."

"Well, he *did* just graduate," Trent offered.

Collin shrugged, "Either you. . ."

"Got it or you don't. I know. I mean some law firms invest in training or development for their new hires. Continued education. Peer training and mentors too. You know, to *teach* them. . .," Trent offered carefully.

"We could try that," Trent suggested, "Find out why he's not meeting your, *our*, expectations and see if we can guide him. It doesn't have to be sink or swim."

"Are we in kindergarten, Trent? Do we need to hold his hand? Why don't you go get his desk and bring it in here next to mine so I can babysit him all day?" Collin said, his voice rising. Trent put both hands up in sur-render.

"I'm just saying, Collin, everyone's been new. Everyone has made mistakes. You have to make mistakes to learn from them. We could build a great team if we invested in the people who we hire and train them. . .."

"He can learn from his mistakes somewhere else," Collin said, ending the conversation. Trent took a deep breath, and with one final "Hail Mary," he said, "Collin, have you even *read* the exit interviews? Everyone who leaves says the same exact thing," and before Collin could erupt, Trent turned and left the office. Collin sat back in his chair and laced his fingers behind his head frustrated with Scott and even Trent too. He was surprised that Trent challenged him like that. As the top-producing lawyer and partner, he made it clear that he didn't expect to be challenged. Ever. What got into Trent?

When people don't measure up, you let them go, he thought to himself, echoing the words of his father. *Our job is not to hold their hands. Our job is to hire them to do their job and do it well. We are not their friends. It's not personal. You will only build strong teams if you hire strong, talented people right off the bat,* his father had said after firing another one of his own employees. Collin thought for a second about what Trent said. About training, investing, educating. But he shook his head and stood up. *Either you got it or you don't. And that's a fact.*

After finalizing a few administrative things, Collin walked out of his office. As he walked the narrow hallway to the lobby, he saw Trent walk into Scott's office to talk. Collin picked up his pace a little bit, growing even more frustrated with Trent. He winked at Shelly on his way out and jumped back in his car. He cranked up his Guns N' Roses playlist and set the cruise control. He didn't want to think about Scott or Trent or Amy or law or business for a while. Collin's thought was, "My world would be perfect if I didn't have to work with these weak people who just don't get it."

When he got to the airport, he headed right to the Flyers Club, the airport's most exclusive lounge, and found the perfect table—away from people. He ordered a beer and a burger and took it over to the window overlooking the runway. He popped in his earbuds and tried to zone out, but a seductive text from Jada caught his focus from his other phone he had tucked away. He responded with the drooling emoji, set an alarm on his phone, and then closed his eyes for a quick power nap. Collin loved certain types of people, and he didn't give a lot of people his time or focus—unless they were pretty female people. He couldn't get enough of that.

When the alarm woke him from a dream about eating burgers with Axl Rose, he headed to his gate. Once settled in first class, Collin opened up his laptop and started looking through his emails for résumés. He was going to have to find someone to replace Scott, and he was determined to find the right fit so he wouldn't have to go through the embarrassing ordeal of hiring *another* subpar lawyer. *Either you got it or you don't,* he whispered to himself, and the plane roared down the runway. He was looking for studs just like him. *That* would solve all the firm's problems.

Reflection
Collin doesn't own up to his own shortcomings, often blaming others, and is very uncoachable. His philosophy is *either you got it or you don't.* Reflect on a time in your life when you disproved Collin's philosophy by owning up to your mistakes and remaining coachable.

5

WARM-UP

Alex was up bright and early to catch the shuttle that would take them from the hotel to the golf course. As it was approaching the hotel, he kissed Christy goodbye, and he and Austin took the short stroll over to the shuttle area.

"I feel nervous!" Austin said, sliding into the back of the crowded shuttle.

"Did you know your body reacts the same way when you're nervous as when you're excited? Elevated heartbeat, sweaty palms, butterflies in the stomach. The physical reaction is the same, so it's up to you to decide what you're feeling. Decide that you're excited! It doesn't make the feelings go away, but it helps you experience them in a more positive way," Alex said as he pulled out his sunglasses. Austin rolled her eyes. He always had something positive to say about everything, and sometimes it drove her nuts.

It had been a few years since The Trio had been together. COVID changed everything and turned all of their worlds upside down. They stayed in touch on social media and through their group text, but life and marriage and businesses and babies kept them all busy and distracted.

In college, the three of them were on the golf team together, but what made their connection extra special is that they all majored in business. Because of their busy commitment to golf, they often took many of the same classes together, further uniting The Trio. They all took Professor Mr. Hightail's Cultivate: Business Fundamentals for Business Leaders class, and all three were eager to unlock the secrets of entrepreneurship, make millions, and change the world.

Cultivate: Business Fundamentals for Business Leaders became Alex's favorite class, an experience that he swears by to this day and credits for most of his success. But Bobbi and Collin thought Mr. Hightail was weird and his class was hokey. They preferred the hard-core business classes, but Alex, for some odd reason, loved this one class, and Mr. Hightail became his favorite teacher. Alex could still clearly remember that first day on the historic college campus and the first day of class.

"So now how did you first meet The Trio again?" Austin asked, using her fingers as air quotes. She had heard a lot about her father's friends and was eager to meet them, especially Bobbi. Austin was about to start many of the same college courses her dad took as a college student, and she wanted all the insight she could get. She was especially looking forward to hearing about the business experience from a female perspective.

Alex smiled as he thought back to the first time he met Collin and Bobbi.

Alex explained that he was the first one at the golf complex for all the incoming freshman golfers. *If you're on time, you're late.* The men's and women's programs worked out together, and they shared the same coaching staff and facilities. He talked about hearing Bobbi before he ever saw her, her loud and distinctive laugh announcing her arrival. He remembered how her bright neon spandex workout gear contrasted against the school colors, how her hair was in a high ponytail, and a duffle bag was thrown over her shoulder, an early indicator that Bobbi had her own style and gave no thought to school colors. *Who wears spandex to golf practice?* Alex asked himself, adjusting his name-brand golf polo that he had ironed just for this occasion.

"I remember the look on her face when our coach handed out our workout uniforms," Alex continued. "Bobbi was not impressed with the color coordination of blue and white, and you could tell she was annoyed because back then there was no such thing as a female cut. The guys and girls wore the same clothes," Alex laughed.

He wouldn't have given Bobbi much thought after that initial meeting, but then she walked into his first class. She moved effortlessly down the aisle and picked the row right in front of him. She put her duffle bag down and turned around to face him. She was relieved to see a familiar face, and Alex was too. Alex also clearly remembered trying his best to look only in her eyes and not at the cleavage that was spilling out of her sports bra, but he left this small detail out of this edition of the story. Bobbi was easy on the eyes and could brighten up a room the moment she walked in. Alex found her to be very engaging and instantly likable, despite her obvious need for attention. As they were chatting, someone plopped down into the seat next to Alex.

"He looked like a model from a golf magazine, was tall, and smelled of the cologne I used to wear in high school," Alex explained.

"It was Collin. He had walked confidently down the aisle and into the empty spot right next to Alex, sat down, and didn't say a word. Bobbi introduced herself quickly, holding out her hand too. Collin shook it." He was less discrete in avoiding the cleavage. Again, a detail that he omitted from this narrative. Alex had this knack for attracting people and was already the glue for the freshman golfers on the first day.

The shuttle had arrived. It was just a short trip to the golf course area right across the street. Austin was the only one in the family who loved all her dad's stories and could listen to them again and again. They both stood up, exited the shuttle, and walked into the pro shop to settle up.

The shuttle driver smoothly exited the parking lot and merged back into the street as quickly as he had dropped them off. Their clubs were already loaded onto golf carts with their name on them off to the left, which amazed Austin. "Dad, when did they grab our clubs? How did they know our names?" Austin whispered, looking around, positive they were being followed. "They grabbed the clubs last night when we checked in and brought them over here either last night or this morning," he explained.

The Breakers was a timeless luxury resort that was gorgeous and modern but had the charm of a historic property that had stood the test of time. Alex always noticed the manicured lawns and the greens. He couldn't wait to see how fast the greens were, the intentionality behind the hole placements, and other landscaping details that he found fascinating. Austin had a lot of patience for his stories, but she drew the line at in-depth conversations about the different golf course grasses you can choose and preferred height of the cut.

"Babe, teamwork makes the dream work. The Breakers is a well-oiled machine. Look around; it takes a lot of people working together to pull this off. Pay attention to your surroundings; look at the attention to detail." Alex gazed over at the landscaping and beauty of the surroundings. He was about to spend the entire day admiring the complexities and beauty of all 18 holes. It wasn't just a golf game he was excited about, but also about carefully analyzing the entire course and paying close attention to how it was constructed, maintained, and uniquely manicured. *You can take the kid out of the landscaping industry, but you can't take the landscaping industry out of the kid.*

"Okay, continue," Austin said, waiting to hear more of the story.

Over time, Collin and Bobbi realized they had grown up in the same social circles. Their parents spent a lot of time and money at exclusive golf courses, country clubs, and golf trips to Scotland. Collin had been a natural golfer since he could pick up a club, and what Bobbi lacked in skill she made up for in sheer determination, grit, and persistence. She was used to being the only Black family at the country clubs, and the only Black girl in many of the summer golf workshops and camps. She earned a reputation for being feisty and vocal, and later her therapist would tell her this was a way for her to be seen when she spent a lot of her life feeling invisible.

Collin over time tried his best to flirt with Bobbi and assumed that one day she would give in to his charm. He had never dated or fooled around with a Black girl, and Collin saw it as a challenge. When all of his usual flirtation techniques didn't work, he figured he would have to change his strategy. But he was confident she'd fall for him. All the pretty ones did.

But Bobbi saw right through Collin and had been around men like him her whole life. She held him off and made it clear that this relationship was and would always be platonic. It took Collin, Mr. Competitive, a while until he truly got the message.

He struggled with this for a bit in college, not being used to rejection. Bobbi had heard all about Collin and his unrighteous ways on campus and wanted none of that.

Bobbi wasn't exactly known for having the best taste in men, but she knew she didn't want to jeopardize a good friendship by falling for Collin's games. Not much has changed. To him, people are there for him to use, and if he can't use them, he moves on quickly. To this day, she is Collins' only platonic female friend.

Alex did not grow up in the same circles at all. When his parents got divorced, a neighbor, Mr. Hank, offered him a position on his landscaping crew that had a contract with several golf communities in the area. Mr. Hank had heard about how the family was struggling after Alex's dad left and wanted to help. Alex wasn't afraid of hard work and woke up before the sun to ride in the van to many of the most luxurious neighborhoods in the city. The yards were huge, and the clients were picky, and Alex was in awe at how the five other guys worked together, almost like a dance. Each guy would start in a different area with a different tool and a different purpose, and sometimes without even a word, they'd quickly move to the next area, change out their tools, and change their methods. The result was a preferred list of meticulously manicured lawns, amazing landscapes, happy clients, and a great tan. These guys could communicate with head nods and quick gestures, and Alex soon figured out this new language and caught on quickly.

Mr. Hank only handled the non-golf course land-scaping and a few homes but knew the ultimate goal was to get a contract to take over the golf course. Getting a course contract and manicure a high-end golf course was like making it to the major leagues for Mr. Hank.

All the years of playing golf and working at golf courses Alex never considered how much teamwork and horticultural knowledge went on behind the scenes with the landscaping crews until he met Mr. Hank and his team. Mr. Hank was from Augusta, Georgia, and when he was younger, he worked on a landscaping team at Augusta National and knew how much went into the maintenance of a championship golf course. Mr. Hank always talked about Augusta; he always used the terms *we* and *us* when telling a story. Alex noticed that. he loved Mr. Hank's stories and thought Mr. Hank almost seemed like a war hero re-living the Augusta experience.

Mr. Hank knew and loved all different types of trees and flowers, but his favorite was the redwood tree, and he had a giant, full-color tattoo of a California redwood that took up most of the space on his bicep. When Alex asked him about it one day, Mr. Hank told him something he would never forget.

"Even though California redwoods are the tallest kind of tree, they have very shallow root systems. These giant trees have roots that go down only 5 or 6 feet," he explained. "The roots spread out laterally and interlock with each other, which is what gives them support. These towering trees don't fall over because they're interlocked by the trees around them."

Alex paid close attention to the feedback Mr. Hank offered his crew on the drive back to Alex's quiet suburban neighborhood each day. He noticed that Mr. Hank would go around the van and mention each worker individually, sharing what he noticed about their work. He was honest and mentioned the details, offering words of encouragement and constructive criticism. When the other guys spilled out of the van at the end of the day, he thanked everyone one by one and would always give them cash for the day. A few days in, Mr. Hank pulled Alex to the side.

"I want to share something with you," Mr. Hank had said, putting his big calloused hand on Alex's sunburnt shoulder. "I have this theory about building good teams. I could hire a bunch of guys who are good with their hands and have experience with a lawnmower, but they wouldn't be able to do what these guys do. I watched each one very carefully before I hired them, looking for specific traits that would help build the team.

They work so well together because they have unique strengths, and they fill in where the others are weak. They communicate effectively, sometimes without saying a word. There are clear leaders and followers, but one isn't better or more important than the other. They trust each other. They keep each other safe. They rely on each other to do their specific job to the best of their ability so the next one can come behind them and do their part effectively."

Alex remembered that as a pivotal moment; it was the moment when he realized good teams don't happen by accident. Good teams need a good coach. After this experience, he looked at every team and organization a little differently. Alex had done all types of odd jobs and knew this was a temporary job and surely appreciated all that Mr. Hank did for him at a critical time, but he knew that Mr. Hank's dream would be to get his own golf course contract one day. He taught Alex the keys to great landscaping are patience and care, and our job was to cultivate each and every living vegetation under our care.

In the beginning, Alex would think to himself, "It's only six of us, and all we do is cut grass. It isn't that deep," but over time he let Mr. Hank be Mr. Hank. He was like a coach, and he treated his team like they were getting ready to take over Augusta National any day now. He could name every plant, every tree, and every bush, and he could look at them and tell you exactly what was wrong with each one if they weren't thriving. Some were overwatered, some were not watered enough, and some were not planted in an area where they could thrive. Some plants and trees thrive in full sunlight, but others need shade. *All these plants are loaded with potential, but it's up to the gardener to care for his garden.*

Mr. Hank taught his team that they must cultivate each part of the landscaping and identify different plants and how to care for them. When you plant a tree and then move it, the root system goes into shock. You need to be intentional to make sure every element in the plant is planted in the perfect place.

"And it's our job to create the right environment so they can become who they naturally are," Mr. Hank would always say.

Mr. Hank took pride in bringing back a plant or shrub from the brink of death. He didn't need an app to figure out what was wrong; he knew from his years of experience cultivating landscapes. It was like he respected and valued them just like they were a real person.

New clients would think that they needed to rip out their landscaping and start over, but Mr. Hank built a brand on bringing an existing landscape back to life and saving the clients thousands of dollars. He'd tell them that **"there was nothing wrong with their landscaping; you just had a bad landscaper."** In a few short months, they'd resuscitate a yard and transform it into the Garden of Eden.

Mr. Hank wanted every tree, every bush, and every blade of grass to stand up and thrive. The same with his people: he never knew how long he would have someone, but he always treated them like family. He took just as much pride in developing his people as he did with his landscapes.

Mr. Hank loved the teamwork it took to keep places like Augusta and Pebble Beach looking pristine. He was once on a golf course crew himself at a local country club but didn't make enough money, so he launched his own company to provide for his family. All of his former employees were young teenagers who needed a summer job and quick money, but everyone was impacted by Mr. Hank. His crew fluctuated between five to seven people, and it never grew past that. Mr. Hank wasn't a real business guy and had no clue how to scale a business, but his team of five to seven people worked as one. He cared for his people, and he cared for his client's yards like they were his own backyard.

"Mr. Hank and his crew had core values they lived and breathed by," Alex explained to Austin. "If you asked any of the guys, they could easily tell you, 'We keep each other safe and use the best tools and proven methods to create gorgeous landscapes, look out for each other, and care about the little details.' That was it. Safety, dedication to excellent service, patience, punctuality, accountability, and attention to detail. The core values of any great company. But the difference was, these guys knew it, and Mr. Hank modeled it. Go into any megacorporation and ask the employees the core values; five bucks says most of them have no clue," Alex said, raising his eyebrows.

"The individual homes we had contracts with became his, I mean our, championship courses. Now, we are done chipping and putting; let's go open up our backs and swing!" Alex said, shifting his focus to the golf course. He waved as a landscaping truck pulled into the parking lot behind them.

As Bobbi and Collin were growing up, the landscape crews, janitors, valets, and entry-level retail workers were insignificant. They were there but not there, necessary backdrops to the scenery. But to Alex, people in these positions were pivotal and necessary. He noticed and appreciated how much work it took to keep this course looking amazing and to provide excellent service. Taking on these odd jobs to make ends meet were life-changing and transformational.

Uniformed staff moved in and out of the impressive building with purpose, taking golf clubs, arranging golf carts, valeting luxury cars, greeting each guest by name, confirming tee times, and keeping the facilities pristine at all times. It was truly impressive and required massive efforts from a lot of people. Easily a couple hundred people just to run the golf course, range, and all the bars and restaurants, working together as one to make sure The Breakers never disappoints.

Alex and Austin were all warmed up and still had no sight of Bobbi or Collin, so they meandered around the pro shop, grabbed some water, and sat on the veranda that circled the pro shop. As they waited, they people-watched for a minute, pointing out that The Breakers was probably the only spot where you would see businessmen in expensive suits get off the same elevator as a lady in a designer cover-up, two men in golf attire, and a family on their way to Worth Ave or the beach. This place is eclectic and full of energy.

Alex checked his phone. It was 9:00 a.m., and according to last night's group text, everyone was supposed to meet at the range at 9:30 a.m. Austin and Alex had been there since 8:15 a.m. because *if you're early, you are on time.*

While they waited, Alex picked up where he left off. "I worked with Mr. Hank for three summers before college, and it really shifted my mindset when it came to building teams and successful entrepreneurship. Mr. Hank was a very small businessman and didn't make that much money, but it really helped me, and it helped my mom keep our family together. I was confused and grew angry after my dad left, but being around Mr. Hank was the perfect medicine. He taught me so much about landscaping, plants, soil, people, and teams. And a family is the ultimate team.

I walked into my business classes already with an understanding of building strong teams, clarifying core values, and making sure your people know them and believe in them. And it is up to the leader to help cultivate *everything.* Mr. Hank took care of his people and his landscapes. Many wayward boys who worked for Mr. Hank went on to be successful businessmen themselves.

"And then you met Bobbi and Collin. . .," Austin asked, gently trying to get her dad back on track to the original story. Alex was notorious for telling multiple stories at once, and as the listener, your job was to make sure you kept him focused so he could finish each story and not leave you hanging.

"Oh, yeah. . .right. Yes. The three of us. The three of us, although very different, worked very well together. We each had our own strengths, and once we agreed on a topic we were all passionate about, each one took our role very seriously. And while Bobbi's rule about never working past happy hour was a little annoying but helped make college fun, and Collin's crude humor, womanizing, and laid-back attitude made me cringe at first, we were able to find our groove as I got to know him. We bonded over our love for golf, business, and horror movies, and we ended up learning a lot from each other. Looking back, I could also see how my strict adherence to a schedule and the anxiety that came from not having a plan was probably seen as an annoyance by the other two," Alex admitted.

Austin's eyes widened. "You? Obsessed with a schedule? Anxious? No. . .," she blurted sarcastically. These were traits Alex still conveyed to this day, and his family liked to tease him about it. Alex rolled his eyes playfully.

"Anyway, what I liked about the group was that everyone was free to be themselves. We built a foundation of a friendship that would last long after we crossed the stage and got our diplomas." Bobbi and Collin had their fans and their detractors, but everyone loved Alex, and he was able to help ease a lot of the social imperfections of his two talented and unique friends.

"Over the next four years, we were inseparable. We called each other the night before we could choose classes to coordinate our schedules. We were on the golf team together. So we have been through a lot; we were there for Bobbi when she broke up with her boyfriend, and then all of the suitors that followed. We went to each other's tournaments, bailed Collin out of jail one time, and they were there when my mom died. We studied together, traveled together, and stayed up till 3 in the morning eating fast-food and talking about how we were going to build multimillion-dollar corporations. That was the pact, that we would be great golfers but also great in business too."

Alex was the natural captain of the golf team while Bobbi, Collin, and the other golfers mainly cared about their individual results. Teamwork was a weird concept for golfers. It was hard to get them to buy into the team concept, but Alex was always there holding everything together, and the head golf coach loved Alex for it.

A loud laugh jolted him from his stories, and he didn't even need to look up to know who it was. Bobbi, in her tight khaki pants, pink polo, gold hoop earrings, and bright pink bag, found them resting on the way to the range. When their eyes met, her face lit up, and she made a beeline toward them. Alex and Bobbi embraced in a tight hug, and then Bobbi turned her attention to Austin. *Tee time is in 15 minutes,* Alex thought to himself. He could feel his anxiety rising. He was happy to see Bobbi but also nervous as hell. *We can't be late for our tee time, and Collin is nowhere to be found.* Alex knew that if a foursome is not ready for their tee time, it can throw the whole course off-schedule.

"Austin! I'm so excited to finally meet you! Your dad has told us all about you. Are you excited about business school?" she chirped, holding Austin's hands in hers. Austin nodded and smiled, and Bobbi plopped dramatically into the chair across from him. *Clueless that she is basically late and tee time is upon us,* Alex thought, fidgeting with the seam of the chair.

They quickly caught up, Alex slightly aware of how Bobbi's voice carried and still, after all these years, unaware of how she draws attention to herself without even trying. He tried not to let the glances of the older golfers bother him and knew drawing attention to her larger-than-life personality wouldn't do any good. She filled him in on how she met Dale, how Jordan was doing in school, and how she "love loved" the people who worked for her. She asked about his wife and the other kids and moved right into work mode.

"How are the stores?" she asked, leaning in, her elbows on her knees, paying close attention. Alex shot a glance at the clock and toward the sliding glass doors at the front of the building. Still no sign of Collin.

"Good, really good. We got some new people working there and the team is really. . ."

"That's so good," Bobbi interjected, "I knew you'd be great at that. I know what it's like to have a strong team. We've done some restructuring ourselves, trying to give the company a fresh feel, you know?" She continued, explaining how each department had changed over the last few years. She wanted to learn from Alex, but her need to talk about herself took over.

Her long-winded explanation stopped only when she caught a glimpse of Collin running into the pro shop. It was hard to miss him, in his aviator sunglasses, teal and orange checked shirt, white golf pants, and designer golf shoes. Alex noticed how Collin lowered his sunglasses a little to get a better look at the checkout girl as he settled up his green fee. Then he did a not-so-subtle double-take her way as he walked through the door to greet the group on the veranda. Collin greeted Bobbi with a firm hug and Alex with a crushing handshake. He turned his attention to Austin and shook her hand.

"Can't wait to tell you all the stories your old man won't tell you," Collin joked, sitting down in an adjacent armchair and crossing his legs. Alex quickly glanced up at the clock. 9:27. Collin noticed and slapped Alex on the knee twice.

"Worried about the time, buddy? This one," he said, gesturing to Alex, "always so punctual." It brought Alex back to the days when they'd tease him for his mini panic attacks if they weren't early for everything.

"Well, we did say 9:30. . .," Alex joked back, waiting for Collin's response. Collin put his hands on his knees and stood up quickly.

"If the gang's all here, let's go warm up" he declared, as he headed toward the golf carts. There was no time to warm-up! Was he joking? Alex felt his stomach tighten and his heart start to race.

"Nope. . .nope, we don't have time, Collin. Let's go to hole #1," Alex said, brushing past the group. He knew they were probably snickering and rolling their eyes behind his back, but he didn't care. There is just something about being late that sent him over the edge, and he wanted this to be a good day. Alex led the group out toward the golf carts that were lined up perfectly.

"Ladies. . .," Collin said, dramatically stepping aside and slightly bowing, gesturing with his open palm and extended arm for Austin and Bobbi to take their golf cart.

Collin jumped into the driver's seat of the second golf cart, and Alex, trying his best to calm down, sat in the passenger seat. Alex took a deep breath. He had put his clubs behind the steering wheel to indicate that he had every intention of driving, but Collin either ignored that or didn't care. Austin turned around from the golf cart in front of him to face her dad. "It's okay," she mouthed and imitated taking a big, slow breath. She knew her dad was struggling and wanted him to know that she was there to support him. He took a deep breath and felt a little better. And knew that Collin and Bobbi loved to rattle his cage, and they knew exactly how to do it too. They secretly loved every minute of it.

"You're going to love college. I learned so much," Bobbi said, patting Austin's knee and pulling her attention away from her dad.

"Yeah, I'm sure you've already learned a lot from your dad. Successful guy, this one," Collin called from behind, elbowing Alex playfully. Austin liked the way Bobbi and Collin seemed to look up to her dad; it made her feel proud. He's so unassuming and rarely brags about himself, but to see these two show so much respect was a testament to how her dad was viewed by his peers. And she could tell that Collin and Bobbi were almost exactly like her dad had described.

"She's got a promising future. She's smart and determined and has great ideas. She's a hard worker. It's so cool she gets to spend the day with us. It's like merging the past with the present," Alex said proudly to Collin, but Collin just nodded. Feelings and sentiments weren't really his thing. Alex nervously waited for Bobbi to take off as she adjusted her hat and checked for her pencil and scorecard.

"Let's teach her everything we know," Bobbi said excitedly, and before anyone could say anything else, she hit the gas, and Collin followed. With a jolt, in real life hole #1 is real close. The four of them headed down the cart path way too fast as hole #1 was only yards away. Their energy and excitement for the day was obvious.

Reflection
Mr. Hank filled his team full of people with varying strengths. What is the value in this? How does that play into what he taught Alex about redwood trees being strong because of their interlocking tree roots?

6

FIRST TEE

They greeted the starter at 9:32 a.m., and Alex apologized for being two minutes late. Luckily, the foursome ahead had just launched their tee shots, so they had a few minutes to wait until they could let it rip. This foursome was made up of three Division 1 golfers and Austin, who was good enough to play at that level herself but chose school instead.

"So, what's our goal here? Or should I say," Alex asked, rubbing his hands together excitedly and raising his eyebrows "Our *common goal?*" Alex can bounce back quickly from almost anything.

"So we're just gonna jump right into it?" Collin asked, pulling a golf club out of his bag. "I don't need to warm up; it's like riding a bike for me. Am I right?" he asked, looking at Bobbi. She rolled her eyes and smiled, as Austin looked back and forth between the three of them, trying to figure out what they were talking about.

"Isn't the goal for me and Bobbi to crush you guys?" Austin questioned, smiling over at Bobbi and asserting her own personality into the group.

"Ah. Yes. That's the goal for the *golf* game. But what I think your dad was trying to do was dive right into one of the first concepts we learned about in school. . .," Collin suggested. Alex nodded, clearly very proud of his creative introduction. *You always start with a common goal. That's the foundation of any successful team.* If you don't prioritize this fundamental, you don't have a team.

"Every successful leader has mastered how to get their team to work toward a common goal," Alex explained. "It seems obvious, but you'd be surprised at how many leaders think their teammates are working toward the same thing, but if you get down to the nitty-gritty and ask them, that's not always the case. Jim in accounting has his own goal, and Susie in marketing is working toward a totally different goal. It's not effective."

Austin nodded.

"Like for example," Bobbi interjected, "I had a department head meeting with all of my managers the other day. We were discussing goal setting, and as I went around the room, I had each person define the goal we were working toward. I was surprised that each manager had a different answer. So we scrapped all the other items on our agenda and took the time to focus on our common goal. This required some of the managers to go back and make some changes in the way their team was working. This focus session helped us get back on track."

"Sounds like you helped them *define their goal,*" Alex said, emphasizing the last phrase.

"I'm pretty sure your dad has all of the notes we ever took in business school memorized. I do remember that part of getting your team to focus on a common goal starts with defining it. And I think the next one was. . ."

"Actually, Collinstop right there. This is the perfect introduction to a little surprise," Alex said excitedly, pulling out his phone. Bobbi smiled knowingly.

"Scan this," he said, holding out his phone to Austin. A black-and-white QR code took up the whole screen, and Austin hovered her phone over it. Instantly, a file popped up on her phone.

"Cultivate Business Fundamentals?" Austin asked, confused, as she scrolled through the file.

"No way, dude. . .," Collin exclaimed.

"These are my Cultivate Business Fundamentals for Business Leaders notes. I kept them. . .," Alex said proudly.

"You kept those?" Collin questioned, now hovering over Alex's shoulder and looking at the phone.

"I kept these," Alex continued, "I had Bobbi turn them into a file so I could share them with Austin. I was going to give Austin the whole binder because I still have it, but she recommended doing it this way instead."

"Good call," Austin said to Bobbi. Bobbi winked.

"These were fundamental in shaping me and my vision for business. I refer to these often, still. Professor Hightail may have been a little whacky, but he knew business. And he knew what the real business behind the business was really about. I kept these, and I want you to have them," Alex said softly. "That was my favorite class; it just made so much sense to me."

She noticed the handwriting right away. Even on her phone, she could see the slight yellowing of the original notebook paper that the notes were on. As she scrolled through, she saw words bolded, circled, and highlighted. She admired a few doodles in the margins and noticed how every page was dated in the top-right corner. He was meticulous back then too.

She knew this gift meant a lot to her dad, and when she looked back up at him, he was gazing at her hopefully.

"I love it, Dad. Thank you. I know these will help me as much as they helped you." She held the phone to her chest and hugged her dad.

"So, if you look right here. . .," Alex said, looking at his own device. "This is what we were talking about," he said, tapping his finger on the words "Get *them involved*" in the middle of the page. "It's easier to get people to buy in if you keep the overall goal front and center at all times. It creates a shared fate. Until you have a shared fate, you don't have a team. We all must be focused on the same goal; you win as a team or you lose as a team."

He turned his attention back to Bobbi. "What did you do after that meeting to keep everyone involved? To keep them personally invested in the common goal?"

Bobbi hesitated but stayed quiet. "Everyone needs to own something," Alex explained. "You can't have a building full of renters. You need some owners. When the common goal is the focus, it is the easiest way to get people and to keep your people focused on the right things. You want all your people focusing their efforts on helping the team achieve its goals."

"Like, maybe you could have sent out an email redefining the goal and then asking everyone for the feedback. Maybe encourage everyone to ask questions, share their ideas, or give examples on how they were personally going to contribute to the common goal. . .?" Alex said hopefully. "Or best-case scenario is to create the goals together; that's the best way to get people to buy into them."

Bobbi shook her head slightly. Alex knew what she was thinking. *Hey, aren't we here to play golf? What the heck is all of this?*

"Yeah, I suppose I could have done that. Too bad I didn't have my trusty Cultivate Business Fundamentals binder and notes in front of me to remind me of that," Bobbi said playfully.

"Austin, you'll learn quickly that in the *real world*, we have real issues that aren't theory. Issues that you won't find the answers to in this Business Bible," she said seriously, pointing to her phone. "Those business classes have a place, but my payroll is real. I have to make real decisions in real time that impact real people. Your dad is right; I could have taken it a step further and made sure we hit the point home, that everyone on the team felt personally invested in the goal. Maybe next time," Bobbi said, as she swung her driver back and forth.

It was almost time for them to tee off. Bobbi always teed off from the tips just like the guys. She hated the ladies' tee box. Bobbi could hit a golf ball just as far as most guys and took pride in it.

Alex continued the conversation, "When I first opened the first hardware store, I was so excited to hire managers to help delegate that I didn't pay close enough attention to their leadership styles. We hired this one girl who I quickly learned was power-hungry and clearly didn't know the difference between a boss and a leader. What I tried to tell her was instead of barking orders from the top, it would be more effective to ask for input from the other people on the team about what goals *they* feel would be challenging yet realistic and how to reach those goals. Getting everyone involved in creating the common goals and helping them to use their strengths to get there will help everyone feel more connected to the overall purpose."

"Did she do it?" Austin asked.

"Nope. For her, the distinction of being a leader meant a clear separation between her and the team. She didn't know how to lead; she just wanted to be in charge. The employees didn't respond very well, of course, and not only were we not aligned in our vision, but nobody wanted to be at work. It wasn't a happy place to be."

"So you fired her," Collin assumed.

"Yep. Had to. And what I learned was that even though she had managed stores before and she had the right skills on paper, I wasn't paying close enough attention to how she valued teamwork, people, or goals. It was a hard lesson, but I'm glad I learned it early on. And she also taught me how important it was to *eliminate distractions*," Alex finished, again with an emphasis on the final two words.

"That's another one, " Bobbi clarified. "See when he does that thing with his eyebrows. That means it's important."

Austin smiled and Alex continued. "Another part of coming together with a common goal is eliminating distractions. Once the team knows what the common goal is, it's important to cut out any jobs or tasks that don't directly relate to the goal; you want all eyes and efforts on the goal." Alex didn't have to look at the file to know what it said under *eliminate distractions.*

- If you don't eliminate distractions, all types of petty things take over.
- Common goals unite people; until you have a common goal, everyone is focused on themselves and their individual input, and you don't really have a team.
- A team is much different than a building full of random people.

Alex pulled the golf club up behind his back and brought it down with a clean swoop, pivoting on his toe and watching the ball fly into the distance. Perfect strike right down the fairway. Alex felt good about everything right now: he was coaching his friends, he was warmed up, and his first tee shot could not have been better.

"So, a leader's job is to ensure their team is focused on and working toward a common goal," Austin recapped, placing her ball on the tee.

"You have to define it. You have to get everyone involved, and that's how you eliminate distractions," she said to nobody in particular. The three of them nodded. Austin took her practice swing.

"And don't forget *well, well, well,*" Bobbi piped in. Austin stepped up to the tee, brought her club back, and in an almost identical swing as her father, sent the small white ball soaring.

"Well, well, well?" she asked, sitting back down in the golf cart.

"Common goals have to be well-defined, well-communicated, and well-supported."

Alex's eyes lit up again. "I forgot about well, well, well! You're so right, and that's so important. Austin, look for that. It's in there," he said, pointing to the phone.

Austin used the search feature to find what she was looking for and then said, "Aha! Right here! Goals work when you work them. When it feels like your team isn't working toward the same goal, it's usually because the goal wasn't well-defined, well-communicated, and well-supported. And if that's the case, it's your fault."

Alex realized Bobbi knew more than she let on from his favorite business class. Alex was on Cloud 9 right now; he knew putting Austin and Bobbi in the same cart was brilliant.

"Yep. If your team doesn't know the goal or doesn't know how to work toward it, it's because *you* haven't successfully defined, communicated, or supported it. That's where you start to bring unity to your team."

Collin walked right up to the tee box and without even one air swing and no time on the range smacked a tee shot that outdrove Austin and Alex by a good 20 yards. He grimaced as his back tightened but didn't dare let anyone know it.

At this point, everyone had sent their golf ball soaring down the green except Bobbi, as she insisted on playing from the same tee as the guys and going last on the first hole. Collin's ball landed way too close to the foursome ahead, so they had a little extra time before Bobbi could tee off. She had one of the longest drives in the history of the NCAA for women. And although it irked Collin to death, she could hit the golf ball just as far as he could.

"So in summary," Alex said, in his best narrator voice, "We learned that a great leader is focused on getting their team to focus on a common goal.

"And now I'm completely prepared for college. Thank you, everyone," Austin said jokingly.

Alex chimed in one last time as he fully expected an intense day of fellowship based on the conversation at the first hole. "To clarify, I meant to talk about our common goals today about this round of golf. You guys veered this conversation off course, just like Bobbi's tee shots," Alex jabbed playfully. They ignored him because they all knew that Alex had every intention of diving deep into business fundamentals.

Bobbi could definitely strike a golf ball, but sometimes she would swing too fast and her hips would come through faster than they should, and she would slice it. When she would do this in college, the guys would pretend to call Domino's Pizza and ask if they needed anyone to come with a "slice." That inside joke led to them referring to her as Domino's when she wasn't playing her best.

"When it comes to our golf day, what are our goals today?" Alex asked. Everyone was silent.

"Well if you don't have any ideas, I came prepared with a few," Alex said proudly

"Of course you did," Collin mumbled.

"To have fun with friends, to connect; support, and learn from each other; and to compete on the golf course to see who still got it," Alex said proudly. He didn't get the cheers and applause he was expecting, so he simply moved on.

Alex knew he had some ultra-competitive friends, and he was worried that their competitive spirit would ruin the true intent of the trip. Bobbi calmly walked up to the tee box and smacked a beauty right down the middle of the fairway that landed slightly right of Collin's shot. Austin just about lost it.

"Oh my gosh! I heard you could hit a golf ball like a guy, but Lord Almighty! You outdrove my dad!" Austin said, giving Bobbi a high-five. Alex and Collin were speechless. Austin reacted with amazement and joy, you could tell she loved this woman already.

"Hold on to your golf hats, boys, we're just getting started," the ultra-competitive, sassy, and fun-loving Bobbi said as she released the brake and drove the golf cart away like a Formula 1 race car, zipping down the cart path. Alex and Collin looked at each other in amazement but not surprised and just busted out laughing. "Dominos, really! Please don't ever say that again," Collin called out, and he peeled off and headed right down the fairway. The day has begun!

Trait 1: Common Goals
Take action: Write down your team's common goal. Is it well-defined? How is this communicated to your team? How do you support the common goal and the other team members?

COMMON GOALS

A winning team requires everyone focused and working toward the same goal together. Your goal needs to be clear and concise with buy-in and agreement from everyone.

7

MONSTER DRIVE

When they approached the second hole, a beverage cart with the golf club's logo on it was waiting for them. A peppy blonde sat in the driver's seat and waved as they pulled up. Everyone had pared the hole, so there was nothing to report there.

"What a warm welcome!" Bobbi said, putting the golf cart in park. "I'll take one, two, three. . .," pointing at her friends and then looking at Austin, unsure. "Four?" she asked, looking over at Alex for approval.

"Not yet. Few more years." Alex said, looking at Austin apologetically.

Collin said, "Years? It'll be months. Your baby is headed to college in the fall. A few more months, and that's it."

"Three beers and a water," Bobbi said to the beverage cart driver who was already digging in the back of her cooler. Bobbi paid and handed the drinks out to the group. "To good friends, a great golf game, and Alex's trusty Business Bible," she said, raising her beer bottle. They clinked their bottles together, and all four took a swig.

"So Alex, you'll keep score?" Bobbi asked, setting her drink in the cup holder and taking a driver out of her bag. Alex shot Austin a glance, and Austin nodded reassuringly.

"Yeah. I got it," he said, waving the small card in the air. Austin grabbed herself a scorecard.

Collin's phone rang, and he glanced at the screen. He walked away from the group and put the phone to his ear. "Hey babe. . .," Alex heard him say as he walked away.

"What's next in that Business Bible, Austin? I still can't believe he kept it; your dad loved that class."

"We talked about common goals, so the next thing Dad has here is *communication* written in big bold letters, underlined, with arrows pointing toward it. I guess this is important," she smiled, showing Bobbi the screen. Sure enough, the word *communication* was highlighted at the top, and the whole paper was covered in notes, even in the margins. The notebook paper looked more worn than the others, and Austin assumed it was because Alex came back to this page often.

"We've talked a lot about communication in our classes, and it's obviously important in business. In everything, right? You have to know how to talk to people," Austin said, unsure of why there was a whole page dedicated to the subject.

"Right. Communication is key to a successful organization. All teams communicate; it's just human nature, right? It's not about making sure your team communicates; it's about making sure they do so *effectively*. And communication is not just about what you say, it's about—"

"How you say it," Austin interrupted, having heard this mantra from both of her parents throughout her childhood.

"Right. And there's nonverbal communication too, right? Like take Rico Suave over there," Alex said, pointing to Collin who was still on the phone. "Now I only know this because I know him, but see how he's digging his toe in the grass like that? And every once in a while, wait for it...," Alex said, watching carefully.

"There, the hand through the hair. He's smiling, his shoulders are back, he's quiet, he's not very animated, calm. From this, I can tell this is not a business call, but a personal one. Whoever he's talking to, he's invested. He's doing something he doesn't do very often. *He's listening*, another huge part of communication...*listening*! He likes whoever this is and is enjoying the conversation." Alex raised his eyebrows to Bobbi in a silent gesture, and she returned the glance. Collin is married, but they'd never put anything past him. If it's Amy, why would he need to walk away?

"As a leader, it's important to pay attention to both the verbal and nonverbal conversation happening within your team. You won't see all of it, but over time you can train yourself to look for little clues that your team is giving you, consciously or not, about their feelings. Being perceptive is a big part of being a good leader," Alex said. "I love to read a person's body language; it helps tell the whole story."

Bobbi thought for a second about her team. She intentionally held weekly meetings to make sure her team was always communicating, but this conversation made her question how much communication was actually happening at these meetings. And perceptive? Listening? Those were new words for Bobbi.

When she thought about it more, she visualized one of her meetings: was there a lot of nonverbal communication happening? Is this why people would stop talking whenever she popped in on another informal meeting she wasn't invited to? As she mentally pictured the break room, she would see texting, writing, and distractions and her teammates talking intensely, sometimes laughing and joking full of animation, but they didn't bring that same passion into the real meetings. She clearly remembered seeing people leaning back with their arms crossed, avoiding eye contact. She noticed more than once people checking the clock constantly, checking their phones, and being silent when she asked for feedback or input. *Why would a loud break room turn silent whenever she walked in?* Bobbi's mind was racing now, *I always thought it was a sign of respect but. . .maybe not? How well do I communicate with my people?* Bobbi thought to herself.

"Client," Collin said, pushing his phone back into his pocket and rejoining the group. Alex and Bobbi looked at each other again and didn't utter a word, but they both knew what they were thinking.

"So what are we talking about?" Collin asked, taking a swig from his beer.

"Communication," Bobbi and Austin said together.

"Mmm," Collin said, nodding and swallowing his beer. "Let me tell you, a team that can't communicate is doomed. The secret is to get everyone talking, to create a space where people share information and listen to each other. Does the Business Bible tell you how to cultivate that?" Collin asked, pointing to Austin's phone. "Because I'm pretty sure I was absent the day we learned how to do that in class; I totally blew that class off, Alex. And don't colleges hire losers to teach business classes? If they were that smart, wouldn't they be someplace actually running a business?"

"And," Collin added, "Honestly, what do we need to talk about so much? Shouldn't everyone just do their job? What is there to talk about?" Collin sounded sarcastic and inquisitive all at the same time.

"When you're in charge of a team, it's your job to listen twice as much as you talk. That's why you have two ears and one mouth, right? To listen twice as much as you speak. When your team knows you're listening, they'll be more likely to bring problems and ideas to you. And that's the only way a company grows, right? By addressing issues head-on and working through them together. You're not a mind reader. You can't possibly know all the things your team is working on, dealing with, or struggling with unless they tell you. And they won't tell you if they know you won't listen," Alex said, looking over to Collin for feedback, but he was texting again and definitely not listening.

Alex continued, "This reminds me of a story."

"Of course, it does," Bobbi said playfully.

"In college, I worked at this coffee shop on campus. I remember sitting down for the interview and the guy kept saying things like 'We can't wait to have you as part of our coffee family' and 'You look like the coffee connoisseur we've been looking for.' It felt weird. Looking back, it was like he had a list of corporate buzzwords to use and he was trying to use them all at least twice during the interview. The next few steps were chaotic and confusing. I had to go somewhere else to get my uniform, I was told to wait three to six days for my schedule, and I was instructed to meet a group of new hires in a separate location on a different day for orientation. It was messy and confusing and indicative of what was to come. But they had this language that only they understood among themselves.

"I got the call about my schedule. I went to the orientation on the confirmed day and time, but it had been moved to a different place across campus. I got my uniform and started the next day. Let me tell you what a mess the next two months turned into. This team had zero communication skills. And it was run by a bunch of 18-year-old kids, no offense," Alex said, gesturing toward his 18-year-old kid.

"Meetings were optional, turnover was high, there were no professional boundaries, and nobody took the lead. The seniors and juniors who were "in charge" were all best friends and let each other get away with infractions they'd fire a freshman over. Even as a college kid I could see all of the red flags. So I gave my two weeks. This was nothing like Mr. Hanks or any job I had at a golf course. I left that job quickly, because I was used to people talking to me directly setting expectations and everyone working together. I knew right away this job and all those people were crazy. I learned a valuable lesson with the coffee shop job: *all cultures aren't equal, and culture is everything*.

There is a difference between developing a real culture versus faking like you have one. All organizations have a culture whether you try to create one or not. You can't fake culture. The key to creating the culture you desire requires constant *cultivation*! For professionals to thrive and reach their potential, they must be planted in the right culture. If payroll is your biggest expense, you better pay attention to your culture and build it right."

Bobbi and Collin didn't interrupt but looked at each other; Tree Boy is on a roll now.

"A week later I saw this ad on the community bulletin board for a college mentoring program. It was on campus and run mainly by students, but let me tell you, it was night and day."

Alex went on to explain how the interview process was intentional and clear. His role as a mentor was laid out in clear terms, and the interviewer took the time to listen to Alex's questions and provide straightforward answers. The interviewer explained the dynamics of the team and reiterated how important it was not only for the team to communicate effectively, but how they were connecting with the college students they were mentoring. He got a call a day later offering him the job and providing clear details about what to expect on the first day.

The first two days were spent meeting the team and learning the best ways to help new college students assimilate to college life. He watched other mentors spend time with their mentees, offer encouragement, and listen to their issues. During their weekly mentor meetings, communication flowed effortlessly. The senior mentors listened carefully to the concerns and questions of the new mentors, and everyone had a chance to speak and voice their ideas.

"Check the file. I'm telling you, this college mentorship program embodied everything Professor Hightail taught about communication. What does it say?" Alex asked, pointing to the phone, even though he knew exactly what it said. Austin found the page again.

"Teams with strong communication. . .," she scrolled and read aloud:

"Have a free-flowing exchange of information,

"anticipate each others' needs,

"ensure that all voices are heard,

"respect the opinions of others,

"are open to other perspectives,

"are transparent,

"have difficult conversations,

"and listen for understanding."

She looked up to her dad for approval.

"Exactly. I took what I learned from this class and in the mentorship program and applied it to my business."

"Sounds like our family too," Austin offered, which stopped Alex in his tracks.

"What?" Alex said, unsure of what caused Austin's reaction.

"That's what you and Mom do," she explained. "You listen to each other; you listen to us. You always make sure we are open to other people's perspectives. Like when we were kids and we were trying to pick a place to vacation. You told us we were going to have a family meeting and to *bring whatever points we wanted to the meeting to be discussed*," she said, impersonating her dad's voice. "You and Mom are straight shooters, but you guys do listen." Alex was taken aback by Austin's observations. The normal sarcastic tone wasn't there. Austin communicated with respect and delight of what communication skills she learned from her parents and her home culture.

"So we sat down in the meeting, and I came with my list of why I wanted to go camping and Ollie wanted to go to the beach. And you made me listen while he explained how cool it would be to find buried treasure, and then you made him listen when I laid out all the reasons why camping is better. And we both got a chance to talk, and then you and Mom talked, and we were allowed to disagree with you as long as we kept it respectful. I liked that it wasn't just you and mom making all the decisions, but you got us involved. You listened to our ideas. I remember that," Austin said, smiling at the memory. "I wanted my way, of course, but as I got older, I realized that I couldn't always get my way."

Alex was touched. He had no idea that the small family meeting would have such an impact on Austin and that she'd even be able to articulate the benefits of it.

"Which brings us to signs of unhealthy communication," Alex said, pointing to the phone. Austin ran her finger down the screen. Bobbi and Collin stood speechless and just listening at this point, convinced by every word but for different reasons and amazed at Austin's maturity.

"Symptoms of poor communication include. . .

"unmet expectations,

"duplicated efforts,

"conflicting priorities,

"silos and unhealthy competition,

"hiding of information,

"decisions made by the same few people,

"and groupthink."

He watched her face carefully as she processed the list. He glanced over at Collin, who clearly had something on his mind. "Penny for your thoughts?" Alex asked. Collin hesitated for a moment and spoke up.

"That list. About weak communication. Read that again, Austin, would you?"

"Unmet expectations. Duplicated efforts. Conflicting priorities. Silos and unhealthy competition. Hiding information. Decisions made by the same few people, and groupthink." Alex could see the wheels spinning in his head.

"Maybe that's our problem," Collin said thoughtfully. Alex always knew that the reason Collin's relationships failed, the reason his businesses struggled, the reason it was hard for him to maintain friendships, and the reason his marriage was always on the rocks was because of poor communication and trust issues. But instead of pointing it out, he let Collin marinade on the idea a bit. Collin had never been fully committed to anything but himself. Alex knew that Collin would be a hard nut to crack.

"The duplicated efforts thing. That drives me nuts. There are so many times, at the firm, where I go to put something in a file or make a change on a client's billable hours and it's already been done or I can't find the file. A paper was filed with the courts, and we missed it. We have some of the same law clerks researching the same things, and we show up in court unprepared. It feels like we waste so much time. I guess, now that I think about it, it's because we're not communicating with each other about what tasks need to be done and which ones are completed. Honestly, I rarely talk to anybody at work;

I just do my thing and expect everyone to do theirs. I love being a lawyer because it's like being a golfer, you know? You are in control, and you don't have to trust or rely on anybody else. If I do talk, it is with a client.

I've also noticed that one of the main feelings I get when I'm at work is disappointment. I feel like I'm always let down by my team because it seems like they can never meet my expectations that I have for them. I hire them, and they never live up to their résumé. I'm constantly asking myself why they're not doing what I expect them to do and why they seem to be incompetent or incapable. But when I think about it, I don't know if I've ever really sat down and told them what I expected or even coached them at all. I guess I kind of just assumed that they know what their roles and responsibilities are, what I want to get done, and when I want it done. As you said earlier, we as leaders are not mind readers, but neither are employees. When it comes to communicating about my expectations, I guess I could be better."

At this point, Alex was dumbfounded and in total shock. He had never heard Collin express himself in this way. . .ever. And it sounded like accountability, something Collin was not known for. He honestly wasn't sure Collin had feelings or was capable of any introspective thought or self-awareness. This sudden self-reflection almost knocked Alex off of his feet. He tried to play it cool, because he knew if he reacted the way he wanted to, Collin would immediately shut down and shut up. So instead, he waited.

"Now what I'm not so sure about is this whole 'decisions are made by a select few' part. There's no way in hell I would trust the guys on my team to make any important decisions about our business practices or the way we do things. They're just not those kinds of guys. I don't think my people get it or are smart enough to think about how we need to operate. I mean they have these degrees on paper but are idiots to be honest. They're there to show up, bill people, and get paid. I don't even think they're interested in having a say in how we do things. I have more experience in this industry than all of them combined, so it just makes sense that I would make the final decisions and they would go along with it."

"Did they tell you that? Bobbi asked.

"Tell me that they just wanted to do their jobs and get out of there?"

Bobbi nodded and waited.

"Well, no, but they've never really shown any interest in contributing to the policies and practices of the firm. Some of them barely seem capable of doing the work I hired them to do. I guess I just assumed, based on their work and general attitude on the job, that they weren't looking to contribute more than the bare minimum."

"Sounds like a real group of winners you got there," Bobbi said sarcastically. Collin shot her a glance. But Alex agreed. If Collin was working with a group of people who only wanted to show up, half-heartedly do their job, clock out, and collect a paycheck, there's no way he was going to build a strong company culture. Your people are clearly disengaged. And without a strong company culture with your firm, there's no teamwork. And without teamwork, his company would never see the growth that Collin was hoping for. But he wasn't going to get into all of that now. Baby steps with Collin.

"From what you just told us," Austin piped in, "it also sounds like there is a little bit of groupthink going on. To me it sounds like you think that your team will just go with the flow and aren't willing or interested in thinking for themselves, making suggestions, providing feedback, or suggesting improvements to help impact the business. Like, nobody wants to stand out. Nobody wants to be the one that makes a difference," Austin said, posing her comment as a question.

Alex took a deep breath. He was thinking the same thing, but he wasn't sure how Collin was going to react to the question or the 18-year-old kid who posed it. Collin was in a vulnerable place, and it was awkward for everyone. Alex didn't know what to do or what to expect. It's one thing for him to be in this rare mood of self-awareness, but it was another for a young female to call him out. Not one of Collins' lawyers was female. When Collin nodded and reluctantly smiled, Alex exhaled, and it felt like a gorilla just hopped off his back. *Is this a breakthrough? Is Collin finally ready to engage in a mature adult conversation? His*

*success has always been because he is so talented, but it was
time for Collin to grow and put his big boy pants on and lead.*

"Yeah, you know, I think you're right. I think communication might be something we really need to work on.
I forgot all about those notes from class, but they seem
pretty relevant to what we are struggling with right now.
We are losing attorneys left and right. They all look good
on paper before we hire them, but there is some type of
performance gap. Communication is such a huge thing; it's
not something we can just have a meeting about, and then
it all gets resolved. And I hate meetings; they seem just like a
waste of time to me. I don't even know where I would start.
I don't even know if they would be receptive to talking
about it or changing things around the office to improve
our communication," Collin said, sounding defeated.

Bobbi couldn't resist and asked, "Do you hate meetings, or do you hate people, Collin? I think you hate
both." Alex started to sweat. *Oh, Lord. Easy Bobbi*, Alex
thought. *Easy.*

"Are you saying you aren't sure how you would *improve
communication on your team*?" Austin asked, looking down
at the phone, back at her dad, and then over to Collin.
And Alex didn't expect his daughter to rescue the moment
and ease the tension but was thankful for it.

"She did that eyebrow thing!" Bobbi exclaimed,
pointing to Austin. "Just like Alex does! Oh no, you have

created a monster, Alex!" and the laughter eased the tension of the moment even more. Alex beamed, proud of his daughter. Collin rolled his eyes playfully, knowing what was coming.

"Yes, old wise one, please tell me what the magical Business Bible has to say about cultivating better communication on a team, my team." It was official that Collin had some sort of breakthrough or a weak moment, but it was a good thing either way.

Austin dramatically cleared her throat and read aloud: "To *improve communication on your team, you must* make sure core values are consistently communicated and practiced, provide an opportunity for everyone to be heard, create multiple avenues for communication, and know your team." Austin used her free hand to count out each point if she read them aloud.

Alex nodded approvingly. He noticed the other foursome behind their group was looking on, trying to figure out why the pace of play was so slow.

"Core values must be consistently communicated and practiced. . .," Collin said out loud to himself, his face pensive. "I guess it would be helpful to have an idea of what our core values are?"

"We had a guest speaker come on campus a few weeks ago in high school, and he started talking about the importance of core values for an organization. He passed around a compass and told us that core values serve multiple purposes in an organization. They provide direction, like a compass, reminding everyone within the organization of its mission and most important goals," Austin said.

"Right," Alex added. "They create connections among the leaders and teammates within an organization. They create a common sense of purpose that unites everyone in the achievement of the company's mission and holds each other accountable. But just having a set of core values isn't enough. If your, or your team's, behavior doesn't align with these core values, it can cause a lot of problems. **Core values should govern the culture. They should be the guidelines that tell everyone, this is how we roll!**"

"You can say that you're a company that focuses on environmental sustainability, but if you don't recycle and you utilize wasteful practices in your business model, you're not in alignment with your core values. This can lead to a leader's lack of credibility, a focus on the individual instead of the team, a loss of focus, and a loss of differentiation. If your goal is to be set apart from your competition, not having core values or not being aligned with the core values means you're just another average company. Nothing special, nothing different."

Collin did the thing with his lips that Alex knew meant he was almost done with the conversation. Tree Boy had one more nugget. "Healthy communication is just like a good fertilizer: fertilizer was created to help stimulate growth. If you communicate well with your people, they will grow and so will your organization. When they start communicating, then you get cross-pollination. That is when something grows or is stimulated by the introduction of a different element." Everyone was tracking, but Tree Boy was off on a tangent. "You want your people talking among themselves well; cross pollination is awesome for culture."

This was a lot to take in, and Collin was being very receptive, but he had a limit. Alex could talk about this forever, but he knew he was the exception rather than the rule. Not everyone likes to geek out on teamwork practices and the building blocks of business. Alex figured now was the time to draw back a little bit, focus on golf, and give Collin time to process everything they had just talked about. Just the acknowledgment that he needed to work on communication within his team was a big deal.

Collin and Alex came from very different sides of the tracks, but Collin always found it easy to confide in Alex. One night, in a drunken stupor, Collin admitted a very personal and emotional story to his friend.

Collin's high school sweetheart, his first love, cheated on him on prom night of all nights. Collin admitted that he had been so preoccupied with golf that he didn't give his girlfriend the attention she deserved. So, she found it in the arms of the high school's star quarterback.

He explained that after the prom they all went to a secluded spot to hang out, drink, and do what high schoolers do. When he noticed she disappeared for a moment and everyone had been drinking, he went looking for her. And when he found her, she was in the back seat of the quarterback's Jetta, and he had seen what he needed to see. The rejection and betrayal did a number on his confidence, and he withdrew socially from everyone for a while. Even now, as a guy who can get pretty much any girl he wants, he has some serious trust issues, and it's hard for him to be committed to anyone, especially a female.

Not a lot of people knew this story, and Alex was honored that Collin had shared something so personal with him. Because of this incident, Collin approached every situation in a distrustful and accusatory way. During their college years together, Alex did his best to diffuse situations where Collin felt vulnerable because of his trauma that only Alex knew about.

Bobbi picked up on the shift in conversation and offered Austin one more tidbit of advice before settling back into the driver's seat of the golf cart.

"One of the biggest takeaways I have about improving communication on a team is making it easy for people to communicate with you. Some people are scared to bring feedback or criticism to your face but would feel more comfortable doing it over an email or even in an anonymous feedback box you put in a common area. I know a lot of the younger people on my team prefer texting over calling, but the older generation still prefers email or a good old face-to-face conversation. I've made it a priority to create multiple avenues of communication so that everyone can get a hold of me, or whoever they need to get ahold of, in a way that suits them best. Offering this type of flexibility increases the chances that people will come to you with issues, concerns, feedback, and suggestions. This keeps people talking and keeps an open line of communication, which is always good for business," Bobbi explained.

Austin listened and nodded, and then asked, "The last thing on that list was knowing your team. How do you do that? Especially with a big business with a lot of people like my dad's. How do you really get to know everyone on a personal level? Seems like it would be overwhelming."

Bobbi nodded. "Your dad is a people person. That's what makes him so good at what he does. Even though he's got a lot of employees—"

"Teammates," Austin corrected her.

"Yeah, whatever. Employees is how I refer to them. They are my employees, and I pay them. As a female, you must always let them know who is in charge. I get it, your dad knows them and knows them well. But that's because it's important to him. It's not just something that he feels like he has to do; it's something that he *wants* to do.

He knows that those personal relationships are so important to the growth of his business. Technology is a different animal.

"Getting to know people just means listening to them. Asking questions. Paying close attention to their strengths and weaknesses and using those to move the company forward. He's a detail-oriented guy, so noticing little things about people comes naturally to him. It doesn't come naturally to everybody, not to me. But it's something that we can continually work on," Bobbi suggested. Austin nodded again.

"But again, I am in technology, so I don't need to do what your dad does for my business."

"Aren't we all in the people business?" Austin asked with a naive smile and looked right at her dad. He looked perplexed because adding in Austin had taken this day and the dynamics in a whole different direction, and at this moment he didn't know if it was good or bad.

When they arrived at the next hole, Bobbi waved down beverage cart and ordered another round: this time two beers, a gin and tonic, and water. They spent the next couple of minutes talking about everything except business. Travel, weather, movies, favorite TV shows, and must-try restaurants in their respective cities. Collin tried to interject politics, but that was shut down pretty quickly. Alex didn't miss anything, and when Bobbi was drinking gin and tonic, it meant she was thinking. So when she bought the second round of drinks and upped the ante on her beverage of choice, Alex knew that Bobbi was in deep thought.

Austin mainly listened as the trio carried the next few holes just like old times. She loved the way her dad could easily transition from talking about business to raving about his favorite sushi place or favorite pro golfer, and he could name just about every bush, flower, or tree and could tell you exactly what conditions it needs to thrive. She loved the way Collin and Bobbi listened intently to him and how gracefully he moved on every time they interrupted him with an anecdote of their own. She watched him as he listened, always maintaining eye contact, always positioning his body in a way that showed he was interested in the conversation. He asked questions when he didn't understand and always asked them to elaborate when he could tell that they were talking about something they were passionate about.

She wondered if Bobbi and Collin appreciated what a good friend Alex was or how lucky they were to have a friend like him. But she saw it. And she loved him for it. Alex loved people and thrived on people growing. His whole business success was based on growing and cultivating people. She just watched Tree Boy work his magic. Austin wondered how she was fitting into the group and decided to be a little quiet and let them do what they do and monitor Tree Boy and all his cultivating analogies.

Trait 2: Communication
Take action: Do you make it easy for people to communicate with you? Make a list of the ways you communicate with your team. Does this work for every person on your team? Do you need to think of different ways your team can communicate with you?

COMMUNICATION

A winning team requires up-front, open, and honest communication with no hidden agendas. If something is not right, talk about it right away.

8

ACE

Every so often, Collin's phone would ding and notify him of an incoming text message. He'd stop midsentence to check it and respond, or hold up one finger to pause the person who was talking so he could focus on the message in his hand. This drove Alex crazy, but he tried hard to let it go. They were there to talk business and play golf, not text. *Be present,* Alex silently pleaded.

"Let it go," Austin whispered, sensing her dad's irritation and nudging him. He relaxed his shoulders and directed his attention to his golf ball on the tee.

When Collin returned, Alex asked, "Needy client, eh?" and he tried to pretend he didn't feel Austin shaking her head in disappointment. Collin stopped and looked at Alex for a few seconds before answering.

"Yeah, you could say that," he said coolly, sliding his phone into the back pocket of his pants.

"How's Amy?" Alex asked casually, staring at Collin. Collin smirked and looked at Alex. They both knew who the phone calls and incessant texts were from, and they both knew it wasn't Amy or a real client.

"She's good. I don't know, man, marriage is hard. We have our ups and downs like I'm sure you and Christy do. She wants to go to therapy, but I'm not so sure. Not really sure what a perfect stranger could tell us about our marriage, you know? Do we yell and fight and throw things? Sure, but that's a part of marriage. We work it out," Collin said casually.

"That's not a normal part of marriage, Collin," Bobbi spoke up.

"Oh, coming from the one who. . .," but he stopped.

"The one who what?" Bobbi asked, putting her hands on her hips.

"Nothing B, never mind," he said, using her first initial like he used to do back in college. It was a subtle attempt to diffuse her.

"No, no," Bobbi said, approaching him. "Tell me."

Alex held his breath. Bobbi didn't have the best reputation for healthy, long-lasting relationships either. Another dynamic of The Trio was that Alex had to break these two up from time to time with their intense squabbles. When they locked horns, it could happen in a moment's notice, and you better be on guard. Bobbi had volatile relationships in college, and her whirlwind romance with Nate was peppered with alcohol abuse, affairs, and unconfirmed assumptions of physical abuse. When he left her in the middle of the night without so much of a note, Bobbi fell apart.

"Okay, guys, that's enough. We can all agree that to make a marriage work everyone has to be accountable for their actions, right? Collin, I'm sure there are things in your marriage that you've done that you regret or have not been conducive to the longevity of your relationship," Alex said, looking at Collin expectantly.

He shrugged. This dismissiveness, combined with the constant texting, was too much for Alex.

"Come on, man, give me a break!" Alex said, louder than he expected. "No accountability? None? You can't think of a single thing that you've done to contribute to the mess that is your marriage?" Alex said loudly. Collin looked surprised. Alex wasn't one for confrontation, and he was surprised to see Alex so worked up. At this point, they had all forgotten about the goals of the day including Alex. To have fun, learn from one another, and compete at golf to see who still has it. *This day is way off the rails now.* Austin knew her dad was focused on Collin instead of golf because he's a stickler for the pace of play, and he wasn't even noticing that the course was starting to get backed up.

"Weren't we supposed to be talking about golf and business?" Collin asked, pointing to the tee. Alex took a deep breath. This day had turned into a business and life coaching seminar.

Alex knew they weren't focused on golf and were lost in some potentially beneficial "fellowship." All four of them are scratch golfers and didn't even realize they were all on the verge of their lowest scores ever. A couple of birdies and a few pars but not one bogie yet.

A few holes later, Alex blurted out, "Austin, what's next? I think you'll find a page with the word *accountability* on top. Let's talk about that, but pertaining specifically to only golf and business of course," Alex said defensively. Austin avoided eye contact and focused on the phone. She had no idea that The Trio could get so intense.

"Accountability is doing what you said you were going to do," Austin read and then looked up at her dad nervously.

"Right. It really is that simple. As a leader or as part of any relationship, trust is the foundation. If your teammates don't trust you, you will never have the company culture that you need to succeed. Blame is the opposite of accountability. When we blame others, we not only relieve ourselves of all responsibility for making things better, we almost always lose trust with the one we are blaming."

Collin's phone dinged again, but he ignored it.

Bobbi out of the blue said, "I have this guy who works for me, Johnny. Nice guy, super good with computers, but is consistently missing deadlines. He misses them by a few days or so and usually has a pretty good reason why he finished his part of the project. I had to have a meeting with him the other day and remind him that he is a big part of our team and that his contributions are required for us to deliver a finished product. He definitely struggles with accountability. He never apologizes, and I never really see him make an effort to get things done on time.

"Before I left I was like 'Hey, Johnny, sorry to be such a pain about this, but are you confident that you're going to be able to get the coding done before I get back?' And he said he would, so we'll see. . .," Bobbi said, shrugging.

"Can I offer my feedback about this particular situation?" Alex asked.

"By all means," Bobbi said and stepped back a bit.

"One of the first things I noticed is that you're apologizing to Johnny for asking him about his role and responsibilities. That's nothing to be sorry for. That's your job as the leader of that company to ensure that everyone gets their tasks and responsibilities completed on time. You're holding him accountable, and there's no reason to be sorry about that. Next time, ask him plainly what he's doing to ensure that his part of the project will be done by the deadline," Alex explained that using terms like "Sorry to be a pain" is about as passive-aggressive as it gets. Bobbi isn't and shouldn't be sorry, and she surely isn't a pain.

"Also, if Johnny continues to miss deadlines, it's because he's been given the freedom to do so. The first and second and third times he missed something, the consequence must not have been enough to keep him from doing it again," Alex explained.

"I guess I didn't really have a consequence. I thought that my disappointment would be enough for him to get his butt in gear. But it wasn't. I just told him that he needs to be better and that it can't happen again. I think he likes me, so if you like your boss, that should be enough for you not to disappoint. And we've had a lot of turnover, and I can't afford to lose anyone else," Bobbi said.

"Your people aren't leaving because of accountability; you've got something else going on I bet. High achievers love accountability. So when he doesn't deliver, what do you do?" Alex asked.

"Nothing really. I asked another one of my techs to pick up the slack," she said, sounding embarrassed. Alex let her think about her situation.

"So you're right, Johnny is not accountable for holding up his end of the bargain when it comes to producing a final product. But you're also not holding him accountable. You're letting him get away with falling short and then on top of that adding more work to another employee to balance out his shortcomings. This is a detriment to your team and your company goals and morale.

"I know you want everyone to like you, and I know it's hard for you sometimes to confront people or have those hard conversations, but you're not doing your team any favors by letting him get away with this. Yeah, he may be a nice guy and he's good with computers, but if he isn't doing what you hired him to do and if he's not showing any effort in changing his habits and behaviors, he may not be the best fit for your team. I'm not trying to tell you what to do, I'm just saying that as a leader you have to be accountable too. Letting Johnny get away with subpar work is not fair to the other techs on your team who are doing what you expect of them," Alex said.

"Says here that accountability is objective. It is truth-telling without judgment. It is solution-focused forward-thinking," Austin said, holding up her phone.

"Exactly. You can pull Johnny aside and tell him the facts. It's not mean, it's not judgmental, it's just the facts. He has been late or missed a deadline this many times, and you've given him this many chances. It's an opportunity to tell the truth, even if it's hard for him to hear. It's also an opportunity to come up with a clear strategy for how you're going to move forward and make it very clear about what action steps will have to be taken if he continues with the same behavior," Alex said.

"You make it sound so easy," Bobbi sighed.

"It's not comfortable, but it's important for the growth of your business. You can't keep people on just because you don't want to hurt their feelings. You have to be an accountable leader. People are looking to you to do what you say you're going to do. Bobbi, you have always been an 'I'll do it myself' kind of girl, so I wonder if Johnny slacks because there is no consequence and he knows you will get it done with or without him anyway. If that is the case, you will lose your high achievers, and the only people left are the slackers who don't want to work hard or be accountable."

"Honesty," Collin added

"What?" Alex said, shifting his focus.

"Our marriage. The truth is that I haven't been honest with her. I haven't done what I said I was going to do. I haven't been accountable for the way my actions have made her feel."

Alex nodded, again shocked by Collin's vulnerability. *We are 43, and maybe this man has finally grown up*, Alex thought.

"And at work, when things go wrong, I'm quick to look for the ways everyone else has messed things up. It's easier for me to blame them for their shortcomings or their mistakes instead of maybe realizing that I set them up for failure or didn't coach them right. I'm inconsistent with my expectations for them, which means I don't hold them accountable. They don't trust that I'm going to do what I say I'm going to do, and therefore they don't do what they say they're going to do," Collin said quietly, fiddling with the grip on his golf club.

Again, Collin's self-awareness surprised Alex. His ability to not only admit that he is playing a key role in the demise of his marriage but also that he can see where he's lacking accountability in the workplace was a big deal. But, like before, Alex let it go. He knew if you push Collin to dig deeper into these thoughts or feelings, he would just shut down. But acknowledging it was a big step, and Alex was proud of him for it. Alex had only one day, so he wanted to be as aggressive as possible without doing too much.

"The last thing on here says that you earn the right to hold people accountable. And that accountability is not one-size-fits-all," Austin said, her finger moving across the screen.

Collin's phone dinged again. He took his phone out of his pocket, read the message, and slipped the phone back into his pocket. Alex pretended he didn't see Collin look at him for approval.

At this point, Alex was officially holding court. *Account-ability*. He could remember the day Professor Hightail talked about it like it was yesterday. He remembered furiously writing as the professor casually dropped golden nugget after golden nugget of priceless knowledge that would eventually lead him to success:

Accountability is what everyone needs to grow and mature.

Accountability is like a great compost full of nutrients added to the soil, and the lack of accountability is like Round-Up. The lack of accountability will stunt a person's growth.

Tree Boy couldn't help it; he saw everything like a landscaper. He made his points and his analogies were a bit much, but they were memorable. Alex and everyone else were starting to realize why Alex loved the Cultivate class in school. Alex saw the people who worked for him like flowers in his garden or trees in his yard, and his job was to help them grow as individuals and to get them to work together as a team. **Alex saw his company as a collection of 150 gardens and he was the master gardener.**

The golfers got back in their golf carts and headed to the next hole. The drive was quiet, almost as if everyone was taking in all of the information they'd learned thus far. Alex liked the silence; he appreciated quiet times of self-reflection. He tried to teach his kids not to be the ones who always felt like they needed to fill the quiet space with random chatter. A lot of people were uncomfortable with silence, but not Alex. He noticed the girls' cart was quiet too, which he hoped meant Austin was practicing the same quiet self-reflection.

He knew the moment would be short-lived because Collin was not comfortable with silence. You could always count on him to hum, whistle, crack a joke, or make some insignificant comment when he felt uncomfortable. Accountability hit him hard, and it needed to; Collin had the potential to be a great leader because he was the most talented person in any group he was a part of. But selfishness and pain have been working against him his whole life.

Alex looked down at his own scorecard, studying it carefully. There were a few spaces that were scratched out and rewritten, and if he looked too long, the numbers seemed to flip-flop. He made a mental note to check Austin's scorecard at the next hole, while Collin reached down and turned the radio up. He started singing loudly and drumming on the steering wheel as they navigated the green, and Alex smiled at how well he knew his friend. Something different was happening today, and he hoped it was for the better.

"We finally are at the turn! 9 holes down. Let's take a quick potty break," Bobbi announced, stepping out of her cart. Everyone ran to the restroom and grabbed another cold beverage. They were only halfway done with their round of golf, but still loads of conversations were left about business and leadership. The conversations were intense, and the foursome each had their best front nine ever.

Austin yelled out the front nine scores before they proceeded.

"Alex, 36.

"Austin, 40.

"Bobbi, 35.

"Collin, 33."

Collin was on Cloud 9 now, especially since he was up and winning. Being the best was where he felt most confident. But Collin still struggled to comprehend how to lead and how teams operate. Collin couldn't understand why everyone couldn't be a stud like him and just do their job. Alex was worried that it was enough to distract his narcissistic and volatile friend from the powerful conversations they had been having.

He had been praying for Collin to grow up for years, but Alex was the only one who knew the backstory as to why Collin struggled with people. Alex thought about letting up because that front nine was the most intense conversation The Trio has ever had. He didn't want to jinx it. But Alex was relieved once he saw Collin strut back to the golf cart. His great front nine kept him focused and happy, which meant he might just be able to hang in there and work toward their common goals: to have fun, learn from old friends, and compete to see if they still had it. Alex smiled as Collin yelled out, "'Hey Austin! Next, what's next?"

Trait 3: Accountability
Take action: List the people on your team and what they are accountable for within your team. Reflect on each person and their responsibilities. Do you hold them accountable in a meaningful way that moves the team forward toward accomplishing your common goal?

ACCOUNTABILITY

A winning team must consist of teammates who can own up to and admit mistakes without blaming others. Ownership starts at the top.

9

THE ROUGH

"Trust," Austin said, scrolling through her phone. "Ah, my specialty," Collin sarcastically sighed while winking at Alex.

"What does it say, Austin?" Alex asked, even though he already knew the answer.

"There are a lot of bullet points here, Dad. You must be reliable. People want to feel safe and secure. Are you someone people know, like, and trust? But if they get too safe or too secure, they might not work hard," she said in rapid-fire succession.

"Hold on, hold on," Alex said, holding up his hands. "Let's take them one by one. The first one says. . .?"

"You must be reliable."

"To build trust in the first place, a professional must be reliable and consistent with their performance," Alex said. Collin just looked blankly into the sky. "I am extremely reliable, so everyone must trust me. I am the most trustworthy person here." Alex wasn't sure if he was joking or not.

Suddenly Austin interrupted the awkward silence with a breath of fresh air. "People want to feel safe and secure."

"Right. That's what trust does, right. It gives your team safety and security. It allows them to do their job because they trust you to have their back—that you will do what you say you're going to do.

"How is trust different from accountability?" Austin asked.

"Great question. So glad you asked. Trust is something we develop with people over time. Or give it to them until they violate it. There is no relationship without trust. The moment that trust is violated, the relationship is in trouble. But when trust is there, you can move mountains. Trust in each other is the foundation of a great team. In life, most people talk about winners and losers, but few people talk about champions. If a team wants to be the best, they must develop high levels of trust." It was like Alex was back in class teaching the Cultivate course himself.

"Accountability is an individual trait to me. Each person needs to be accountable to themselves so they can grow and mature but also accountable to the team to do their job so the team can win. Trust requires others to be involved. You can be accountable all by yourself."

"I like that!" Collin chirped. "I can be accountable, and I don't need someone else to do it with me. I'd like them to be accountable to me but most importantly themselves, but trust requires reciprocal trust for it to work. We must trust each other," Collin added. It seemed as though he was back from his emotional abyss.

"Are you someone people know, like, and trust?" Austin said, reading the next point.

Alex, responded, "A few years ago I met a guy named Jack. Jack came rushing into store #6 in a panic. He had just started his own construction company and was in the process of ordering lots of expensive tools to get started. He put an order in with a hardware store down the street that won't be named."

"Was it Murphy's?!" Collin asked, wanting all the juicy details.

"He put an order in with a hardware store down the street that won't be named, and when he went to pick up his order, there was a disconnect. Nobody at the store could give him any info about his order. They sent him on a wild goose chase to three other stores and still didn't have any information about his order. And the worst part was, the employees didn't seem to care. There was no sense of urgency and no real worry or concern about how their mistake would impact Jack. No accountability. All the store employees cared about was not getting blamed for the mistake. And none of them cared about Jack or his business. Thankfully, Jack didn't pay anything yet and wasn't out of money, but he needed his tools desperately or he would be.

"So this leads Jack to our store for the first time, overwhelmed and desperate. Jack and I had talked a few times at different community events we attended together, and his wife and Christy do yoga together. Store #6 went into overdrive, looking over what he needed and going above and beyond to fill it. If we didn't have the tool, one of the teammates drove over to another store to get it for him. We made phone calls; we did it all. This was before the Internet. All we had was old-school yellow pages and our own inventory. By the end of the day, Jack had all of the tools he needed in time to start his build." Alex looked around, smiling.

"We aren't in the hardware business; we are in the people business," he finished. Collin and Bobbi both looked up and were fixed on Alex and every word. Alex knew he was back in charge and holding court. He also felt like the day was back on track. All he wanted was for his dear friends to learn how to cultivate their people the same way Alex had been cultivated throughout his life and was cultivating others. It was his full-time job. Alex knew that this could help both Bobbi and Collin in their personal lives too. Neither of them had any idea that Alex was dyslexic. He figured today may be the day he'd tell his friends about his little secret.

"Guess who now has a multimillion-dollar building company and comes to us for every single screw, nail, hammer, lumber, and piece of wood?" Alex asked, proudly.

"We showed Jack that he could trust us. And, lucky for us, the store that shall not be named showed they didn't care about Jack the person. From then on, Jack knew us, liked us, and trusted us. We've earned his business for life because we were someone he could trust when he needed it. And all his construction friends now come to our store as well. I can't even calculate how much money we have made just off Jack or his referrals. My people know we are in the people business, and we must take care of our people internally and externally."

Austin nodded, satisfied with the answer. Bobbi and Collin stood quietly, hanging on every word.

"But you said earlier that trust goes both ways," Bobbi said thoughtfully.

"Right. Your team is accountable for what they do, but they have to know that you trust them. One of the biggest ways to let your team know you *don't* trust them is by micromanaging them. Working over their shoulder, completing work for them, obsessively checking in, and mandating that you are part of every decision is screaming 'I don't trust you' to your team. And when they don't feel like you trust them, they feel like—"

"Renters," Austin piped in, and Alex shot her a look. He wasn't expecting that from her, but she was absolutely right. His daughter was growing up hole by hole, and it was the perfect piece to this golf day. A chip off the old block.

"Renters," Alex confirmed. "If you don't trust them to do their work, they won't feel a part of a team or know how they contribute to victory. They won't find joy in their jobs, and they won't feel like they're a valuable part of the team. A lack of trust causes stress, and stress does not equal productivity over the long haul. I mean, everyone needs to own something. It's the only way to create team pride. My people know how they contribute, there is no confusion, and they know I could not have done it without them."

Bobbi turned to Austin. "One of the ways I try to build trust with a client is by always telling them everything I *will* do. When we sit down the first few times to discuss our goals, I always tell them what they can expect from me and what we can promise *not* to do. I make this very clear up front, even put it in writing, so that they have clear expectations. And as our professional relationship develops, they notice when I do what I said I was going to do and when I don't do what I say I wouldn't do. Like surprise fees or changing the contract without them knowing. Over and over again I stand by my word, and this builds trust."

Alex liked listening to Bobbi explain her thoughts to Austin. He knew sometimes getting a lot of information from her dear old dad could be overwhelming, and he was thankful for the fresh perspective.

"Do you do that with your teammates too?" Austin asked. Bobbi stopped to think. Alex waited.

"No. I mean, that's not a conversation I've ever intentionally had with my team. My focus is on my client, because my reputation is on the line. I built this thing from scratch, and I would never let someone ruin what I have built. Maybe it's harder for me to define what I will and won't do when it comes to them. My role with them changes. I don't want to say 'I'll give you creative freedom on this project' because they may not do it right, and I'll need to swoop in. . .," Bobbi trailed off, realizing what she was saying as she said. Alex raised his eyebrows.

Alex chimed in delicately as Collin listened intently. "Bobbi, you know I love you, but I counted how many times you said *I* or *me* or *my*. Those words are very dangerous for a business leader. I even teach our kids—"

Austin finished the sentence. "I, me, and my are a three-headed monster."

Alex nodded proudly and continued. "It is so critical for a business leader to use the terms *us* and *we*. It is subtle, but it's huge for the sake of your culture. I realized early that if I was ever going to be a great leader, I must look at my leadership differently. My people don't work for me; they work with me. We are teammates."

"I turned into a monster," Alex said honestly. "*Me. . .my* all day long. Mr. Hank taught me well; I learned a lot about the team mentality at the country clubs and golf courses I worked for growing up. But I failed miserably in the beginning because *my own money* was at stake, and I couldn't let my business fail. In my mind, I had spent my last dime on this hardware store and everything I earned in my short-lived pro golf career was on the line," Alex said softly.

"It was only three of us in the beginning, but guess what, once Christy left the store and left it to me to run, I realized it takes only two people to make a team. I got my ego out of the game a long time ago. I am ashamed I let money or the fear of losing change me from who I was." He realized he had gone off of a tangent and brought the conversation back to Bobbi.

"So if your team doesn't know what to expect from you, it probably makes it hard for them to. . .," Alex said waiting for Bobbi.

"Trust me," Bobbi said quietly. Alex nodded. Austin gave everyone a second to soak up the moment before she read the next bullet point. "A leader with integrity doesn't spend their time telling their team what's wrong; they spend their time telling their team what's right."

Collin let out a loud laugh, and everyone looked at him. "Sorry, sorry. I just, I mean, come on. What are we supposed to do? Walk around and give out gold stars or milk and cookies for people doing their job? These aren't children; they are adults. No news is good news in my book. If I'm not confronting you about how you screwed up, you must be doing all right." Collin looked around the group, scanning faces for validation. He didn't find it.

"It's not about being condescending or having to pat people on the back for doing their job. But who doesn't like to hear praise every once in a while?" Alex asked, surprised at Collin's reaction.

"Managers who publicize and/or ridicule the mistakes of their employees create a culture of fear. Then mistakes become hidden, and blame is deflected. It's impossible to build trust in this type of environment," Bobbi added, looking over at Austin. She nodded.

"Being a leader means cultivating. . .," Alex nudged Austin and raised his eyebrows, "an empowering work environment where people feel seen. When you look for the good, you'll find it. And when you build a reputation for seeing the good and pointing out the positive, your team will want more of that. And then, when something goes wrong, they'll take your criticism as helpful instead of hurtful and will be incentivized to make it work. They'll want to avoid making mistakes not because they don't want to get in trouble but because they don't want to let you down."

This idea reminded Austin of the one and only time she snuck out of the house as a teenager. Her friends pulled up in front of her house, she opened the window having deactivated the alarm earlier in the day for preparation, and sprinted through the front yard to the waiting car.

They peeled out of the neighborhood and toward the lake. She was already tipsy when a pair of headlights came cruising down the dirt road, and she knew instantly who it was.

Most of her friends scattered, and Alex didn't have to say a word. She stumbled into the backseat and kept her head down. He didn't yell. He didn't scream. He simply said, "You are so important to us, and I am so glad I found you. If anything happened to you, I wouldn't know what to do with myself. Are you okay?" Austin remembered bawling in the back seat and then opening up the door at a red light to throw up.

He always pointed out the good. He always made her feel seen and valued and important, and she felt ashamed for letting him down. She didn't get away with it, though. There were serious consequences, and she deserved them. But she never rebelled like that again, not because she didn't want to get in trouble, but because she didn't want to disappoint her dad like that again. It took a long time for them to trust her again, and once they did, she never wanted to jeopardize that.

Austin came back to the present and looked down at her phone. "Okay, this says 'As leaders, there are times where you can't share all the information to which you are privy, nor would it be beneficial to do so. However, we also tend to withhold information for our own convenience when revealing it would require uncomfortable or inconvenient discussions.'" Austin looked up at her dad, expectantly.

"Right. Another aspect of building a culture of trust is first breaking down a culture of secrets. The Dalai Lama said: "A lack of transparency results in distrust and a deep sense of insecurity.""

"Deep," Collin said.

"It's true, though. I'll admit there are things or resources I don't share with my team, and I don't know why. I guess it feels good to have a little bit of info that they don't have. If I'm being totally vulnerable. . .," Bobbi paused, "keeping this information to myself makes them need me.""

Alex wanted to hug her. He knew how hard it was for her to admit this, and he tried to suppress his smile. He was so excited about all of the breakthroughs today. The fact that they were all having an incredible golf game added to his joy.

Trait 4: Trust
Take action: Trust is a two-way street. For your team to trust you there needs to be an appropriate level of transparency. Think through the information your team needs to effectively do their part in working toward your common goal. Are you transparent enough? Too much? If you are under or over transparent with any of your teammates, think through a plan to change this immediately.

TRUST

A winning team is built on transparency and absolute faith in your teammate's abilities and motives. Trust is strongest when everyone values and depends on one another to play their role with complete confidence in one another.

10

EAGLE

"**D**ad. Dad. Don't. Hey! Dad!" Austin said in a harsh whisper, knowing exactly what her dad was about to do. But it was too late. He couldn't help himself, and he was already walking that way.

"Where is he going?" Bobbi asked, standing next to Austin, watching Alex jaunt across the green.

"To talk to the landscaping team," Austin said, sounding defeated.

"About what?" Bobbi asked. Austin shrugged. "Either plants or teamwork. Probably both."

The two men in black pants and soft yellow T-shirts stopped raking the sand when Alex approached.

"Hey, guys!" Alex said excitedly. "Can I talk to you for a second?" He quickly looked back at his group and saw Austin and Bobbi standing next to each other, arms crossed and talking to each other. They've become quick friends. He knew they were probably making fun of him, but he didn't care. The men stopped working, looked at each other confused, thinking they did something wrong, and waited for Alex to speak.

"I know you're very busy, won't take up a lot of your time. Just wanted to let you know this course looks incredible. I have an appreciation for master landscapers like you guys. I mean, look at this place," Alex said, gesturing to the whole course.

"It's a masterpiece. Really. You guys used the lily grass perfectly, and the pentas are brilliantly placed, love their color. It all really makes a difference and enhances the golf experience. And I know the careful attention to detail that comes with creating a green space like this. I know you guys spend a lot of time removing ball marks, maintaining the bunkers, and repairing the divots we miss. Then there is pest control and. . .. I could just go on and on. I just want to let you know that I see you, and I appreciate the hard work," Alex said, becoming acutely aware that he was the only one talking and on the verge of completely geeking out over landscaping.

Alex noticed the confusion on their faces and that they looked back and forth to each other without saying anything. Alex realized they probably hadn't understood anything that he said and that maybe English wasn't their first language.

"Aprecio tu trabajo duro. El campo de golf se ve muy bien. Gracias por todo lo que hacen," Alex said, reciting one of the few Spanish phrases he had committed to memory. As he spoke, he saw the recognition come across their face, followed by big smiles. They all shook hands, said goodbye, and Alex jogged back to his group and hated that he couldn't translate lily grass and pentas.

"What was that all about?" Collin asked. "Why in the world would you need to talk to them?"

"Oh, nothing. Just wanted to thank them for their hard work on the course. This is such a gorgeous course. and I can't stop thinking about all the teamwork and dedication and commitment that goes with maintaining a course like this," Alex said.

"You've always been so good at that. Seeing the people behind the product. I love that about you," Bobbi said, putting her hand on Alex's shoulder.

"What did they say? Did they share their secrets about perfect golf course chemistry?" Collin joked.

Chemistry. Alex thought. He knew this was one of the fundamentals that they hadn't talked about yet, and he was wondering if they would get there.

"Actually, yeah," Alex fibbed. He figured the end justifies the means. "We were in a deep discussion about the different chemicals used on a golf course. Herbicides, pesticides, insecticides. They all have to be carefully applied and perfectly managed to create a course like this. It's easy to look at the golf course like this and forget about how the careful application of chemistry is what makes the greens look like this."

"I hated chemistry," Bobbi mumbled.

"Oh, I loved it!" Austin squealed.

"So Austin, what do you remember about oxygen and hydrogen molecules?"

"We all know the importance of oxygen, but if you want to make water, you need twice as many hydrogen molecules as oxygen molecules," Austin said, thinking back to her high school science class.

"Right! It is absolutely possible to have too much of a good thing! When we hire new teammates, we look for the oxygen-like qualities such as ambition, a positive outlook, and experience in the same type of position, but we also need to consider balance.

"A team loaded with optimism needs someone who will identify roadblocks. A team full of players who charge ahead needs someone to slow things down now and then to make sure critical details aren't overlooked. A team of professionals with nearly identical experience needs a fresh perspective to challenge their assumptions to prevent groupthink."

Alex looked over at Collin and knew he had to shift gears a little bit to get Collin interested in this part of the conversation.

"Collin, what was one of the things that our golf coach was always saying we needed to work on?"

"Remembering that even though we were used to golf being an individual sport, we had to approach it as a team sport. The members of our team were not our competition. I felt like this was a message directed right at me. I had a really hard time not focusing on beating and being better than you guys."

"Exactly! Athletic teams with strong chemistry don't rely on the same players all the time to do everything. They realize that different opponents, courses, injuries, and even different weather conditions, call for different players to step up while others take a step back; a championship team needs everyone."

"Unless you have a stud golfer; then you just use him to bring your team a championship," Collin said jokingly, but they all knew part of him still believed it. Alex let it go.

"The same is true in the workplace. Different internal and external environments call for different responses. Different projects and stages within those projects require different combinations of strengths and abilities. Our job is to recruit, develop, and retain top talent and to get them to work together as a team in harmony together. That is our number-one job as a business leader.

"If you are consistently relying on the same one or two people to lead in every circumstance, you are not utilizing your team to its full potential or achieving the level of results you could be."

Alex watched Collin process this. He knew this was personal and knew that Collin still struggled with feeling like he had to carry his team. He did it back on the golf team, and he was doing it now with his job. He stepped in and did all the work himself because he didn't completely trust anyone else to do it for him. And, letting others step in and do what they're good at made Collin feel inferior and insecure. He had heard a colleague say once that there was room at the table for everyone, that everyone could be their best and could still support each other. But this was an idea that felt foreign to Collin. He felt his familiar *either you got it or you don't* mentality creeping back in.

"Says here that Sir Derek Barton, who won the Nobel Prize for chemistry for research that serves as a critical foundation of organic chemistry, once pointed out, 'Every chemical reaction has a transition state,' Austin said, holding up her phone. "What does that mean?"

"When we begin to experiment with team chemistry, there's often uncertainty as we see changes, a shift, starting to happen. Will it lead to the result we're looking for, or will it explode?"

"I feel like the natural response to this would be to intercede as we see this shift beginning—to adjust it, to accelerate it, or to reverse it. It doesn't feel natural to make a shift that could, like you said, cause an explosion on our team." Bobbi responded.

"But what happens when you do something to change or alter the result of an experiment, Austin?" Alex asked.

"If we make changes or do things to avoid a result that we don't want, we can throw off the experiment in its entirety," she replied.

"Bingo. We do the same thing as leaders. We jump in quickly when we sense a change because we don't want to ruin what we've built. We don't want anything changing what we know works, even if the result could be something better."

This caused Bobbi to think back to a situation a few months ago where she sensed a shift in one of her departments. She knew her team sometimes thought she was clueless, but she was able to pick up on something happening. It happened when she brought in a new COO.

Maggie seemed committed and knowledgeable about the industry, but it took only a few weeks for her true colors to show. She started criticizing the way Bobbi managed her team and on more than one occasion gave the team members excessive freedom and flexibility to complete a project that was approaching a deadline. Bobbi sat in the back of the conference room while Maggie delegated different projects to different people and then completely removed herself from the role. She even brought in a whiteboard that she hung on the office wall with the expectations for the week. Bobbi hated that whiteboard.

One day, Bobbi was walking toward Maggie's office and overheard her having a conversation with her most loyal employee, Craig. She heard Maggie explain to Craig that she was taking time to sit down with each employee individually and have a discussion about how they prefer to be managed. He talked about having freedom, flexibility, and autonomy. He talked about working better when he wasn't micromanaged and that he was trying to be better about setting professional boundaries. He brought up the raise again. *He was obsessed with this damn raise.* He wanted to work in a space where you could come to work, do his job, and not feel like he was on call at all hours of the night. He knew he was good at his job, he knew what he contributed to the team, and he was looking for a manager who saw it too. Craig's answers punched Bobbi in the gut. She let Maggie go that day.

She had called Alex on her way home, overwhelmed and irritated and unsure what to do next. But if she wanted someone to vent to, someone to sit in misery with her, someone to gossip and talk bad about Maggie with, Alex wasn't it. He listened, of course, but when she was finished ranting, he calmly asked, 'Do you want help with this, or do you just want me to listen?'" She said she wanted his help, but she didn't like his answer. At the end of the conversation, they decided that Bobbi's habit of intervening out of fear may have cost her a valuable COO. She had an opportunity to lead her team in a way that would make them happier, more involved, and more productive, but she threw it away. She had the chance to improve the chemistry on the team, but she saw this shift as a threat and neutralized it.

To this day, Bobbi wondered what would have happened if she had let Maggie do her thing. She wondered if having a one-to-one discussion with the employees about the ways they felt most productive and the ways they wanted to be managed would have changed the company culture. She tried not to dwell on the woulda, shoulda, coulda and focused on the present. *Which reminds me*, she thought, *I need to start looking at résumés for a new COO.*

"Bobbi, the last two things in the notes may interest you," Austin said, pulling Bobbi out of her memory. "The first thing says 'The difference between a user experience that creates lifetime customers and one that just gets the job done may be how well the creative and tech teams are working in sync.'"

"And the second?" Bobbi asked.

"The difference between an industry-disrupting product and something that looks a lot like what your competitors offer could be whether your innovative team members are motivated and empowered to contribute fully."

Everyone waited for Bobbi to respond, but she didn't. She didn't have a sarcastic remark or playful jab or smart remark. Instead, she sat down in the driver's seat of the golf cart, pulled out her phone, and started typing.

Everyone waited in silence. She seemed to text forever, her nails clicking furiously on the screen of her phone. Finally, the swoosh sound made it clear that whatever message Bobbi had typed was out in cyberspace.

"What was that?" Collin asked.

"Two things. I emailed Maggie. I asked her if she'd be willing to sit down and talk sometime next week. And I sent a quick email to my techs letting them know how much I appreciated all of their work and told them I wanted to take them out to lunch when I got back to hear their ideas about how we can improve the chemistry in our office, what I can do to manage them better, and what ideas they have to help the company grow. Now," she said, tossing her phone into her bag, "Let's finish this golf game guys. My business is just like a tree, and I am officially in the people business."

Austin shot Alex a look of surprise, and Alex did a horrible job of hiding his ear-to-ear grin.

Trait 5: Chemistry
Take action: Analyze your team chemistry. What is working well? What isn't? Set up a time to talk with each person on the team to get their perspective on the team's chemistry. Truly listen and take appropriate steps to systematically change what needs improvement.

CHEMISTRY

A winning team requires a collection of diverse skillsets and abilities with like-minded individuals creating the perfect synergy. Talent is maximized to leverage everyone's skills for the good of the team.

11

Knee Knocker

Over the next few holes, the group stayed pretty quiet as everyone focused on their amazing day of golf. All four of them were on the verge of personal records on the course. It was as if everyone was reflecting on the deep conversations of the day, looking inward to see how learning this information could change their respective businesses that each of them relaxed and attacked the challenging course. Alex took in the silence. He saw the wheels turning, and as much as he wanted to pick their brains and dive deeper into the discussion, he had learned over time to let the magic happen in the silence. He decided to wait to see if anyone else started up the conversation again, but he was playing lights out too and had a chance to have a lower score than Collin, maybe for the first time ever.

He knew what the next topic was from his notes, now on hole 16. *Commitment.* He knew a lot of people struggled with this concept, but it was always hard for Alex to understand why. When he wanted something, he went after it relentlessly. When he signed up for something, he saw it through to the end. When he gave his word, he always followed through. It was part of who he was, which is probably why flaky, inconsistent, noncommittal people drove him absolutely mad.

His therapist tied it back to his father leaving, of course. It seemed like all of Alex's issues stemmed from there. His therapist helped Alex see that his father's lack of commitment to his family broke something in him, and he tried to fix this brokenness with an almost obsessive level of commitment in everything he did. This apparent family tragedy helped Alex commit to people as much as humanly possible, and it was genuine, something that not many people have ever experienced before.

"....I'll send you the link. They're great shoes. I wore them when I ran my first marathon a few years ago," Bobbi said to Austin, and with the mention of a marathon, Alex saw his way into the next part of the conversation.

"I forgot you did that race," Alex lied, "What an accomplishment! How'd you do it?" he asked, hoping it was enough to get the commitment conversation started.

"Well, I put one foot in front of the other, but really fast," said Bobbi sarcastically. Austin laughed.

"I mean, how did you train for that? Why did you do it? How long did it take you to train for something like that?" he asked, genuinely interested.

"Dale and I love to run, and he's done a lot of half and full marathons. He even did a triathlon! That's not my thing, but I do like the challenge of a good long run. For me, right at around seven miles my body just does it on its own. I just have to work on keeping my mind present."

"How did you train for it?" Alex asked again, trying to steer the conversation to the magic word.

"For a marathon, I gave myself 12 weeks of training time. I set a date to start and dedicated all of my energy and focus to my training. Every decision I made for those 12 weeks was made based on how it would impact my training. I said no to pizza and beer, I ran when it was raining, and I missed bachelorette parties and happy hours. And if you know me, that's no easy feat. But I was committed."

There it is. Alex thought.

"And when you're committed. . .," Alex started.

"Uh-oh. The eyebrows," Bobbi said, pointing to Alex.

"And when you're committed, you will always have consistent actions that line up with your commitment. Your dedication to what you ate and how and when you trained were an outward expression of an inward commitment."

Austin pulled out her phone and scrolled to the next page. Sure enough, the word on the top of the page was *Commitment*.

"When you are committed, you'd never ever quit. When you are committed, you will actually recruit others to join you in your commitment, and you will seek out others who are committed to exactly what you are committed to," she read out loud.

"Eh, I don't know about that. When I was training, I didn't want anyone to be part of my process. I don't like running buddies. I don't like coaches. I don't like having to rely on other people. Whether I ran or not, whether I ate right or not, whether I finished the race or not, I wanted it to because I did it." Bobbi said, sounding defensive.

"Who did you marry again?" Alex asked.

"Dale?" Bobbi said, confused.

"And didn't you say he was an avid runner?"

"Yeah but. . ."

"It doesn't mean you have to run the race together. It just means you surround yourself with people who are also willing to commit to things that are important to them. Would you say Dale was committed to his restaurant in California?"

"Oh, 100%," Bobbi said quickly.

"And would you say he's committed to you? Your family? Your daughter? Your lifestyle?"

"Completely," Bobbi said confidently.

"So it's true. You recruit, in your case marry, people who also value commitment. You guys share the same vision for your life and are committed to making it happen. A good business leader will do the same. You can't expect to run a successful business if you hitch your wagon to people who aren't committed, who aren't going in the same direction," Alex explained.

Bobbi thought and nodded.

"Do your techs know what direction you're going?" Alex asked, already knowing the answer.

"I mean, I don't know. I don't know if we've ever talked about my vision."

"So how can they be committed to your vision if you don't share it with them? The difference between compliance and commitment is how personally connected an individual feels to the outcome."

"Right," Bobbi said, pondering the idea.

My people at Red's know the vision, and it is way bigger than 150 stores and everyone knows it.

"One of the things we learned in my business class was that one of the quickest ways to increase the level of commitment among your team members is to involve them in planning and decision-making processes. Tap into their front-line experience and ask for their input regarding the likely impact of potential courses of action. The more included they are in the process, the more your team will buy into the strategy," Austin added, looking at her dad for approval. He winked.

"It's hard to feel personally connected if you are merely following orders or if you don't understand the purpose of what you've been asked to do," Alex said, trying to sound casual but repeating what was written in the notes verbatim.

"It also says when you are committed, you are willing to make sacrifices and walk away from other things that would distract you from your goal," Austin said, "Sounds like you did that when training for your race."

"Oh, for sure. It was easy for me to do chicken and veggies every day, fit in two workouts a day, and wake up early for a run once I signed up and committed to that race. It was worth it to me," Bobbi said.

"In business, we have to be able to spot the things that are distracting us from our goal and let those things go. Sometimes everything feels like a priority, but being committed means looking closely at what it will take to reach our goal and not taking no for an answer," Alex added.

"Says here that a successful team will be committed to three things: committed to the outcome, committed to bringing your best self every single time, and committed to supporting each other," Austin said, looking down at her phone.

"Sounds like marriage vows," Collin piped in.

"It does!" Alex agreed. "In marriage, we vow to love and cherish each other, to put each other first, and to support and encourage each other, through every season. Both people have to be committed to making the marriage work, be honest and faithful, and be the best version of themselves. Lord knows it's not easy, but that's the only way it works."

Alex knew that so many of his friends meant what they said when they got married, but the skyrocketing divorce rate among people his age was a testament to the fact that many people are talkers instead of doers. It's easy to get up there and pledge this commitment on a special day, but when the trials come, it's hard to put those words into action.

Alex always tried to remind his kids to be doers. Don't say you're going to get better grades this year; put a plan in place, and actually do it. Don't say you're going to be nicer to your sister; actually do it. Don't say you're going to cut off that toxic friend; *do it*. Actions speak louder than words, he'd tell them, and your actions speak volumes about your level of commitment. Think! Execute! Win! It's that simple!

One of the excuses Alex never accepted from his kids or his team was "I didn't have time." When a problem arose and the response was "But I didn't have enough time," Alex would always respond the same way. "It's not that you didn't have time; it's that you didn't *make* time. Instead of saying 'I didn't have time,' replace it with 'it wasn't a priority for me' and see how that feels." Not making time for a particular task is a reflection of your level of commitment. "If it's important to you, you'll make a way. If it's not, you'll make excuses," he would say.

Alex learned the importance of commitment firsthand during his summers working for Mr. Hank. The yards didn't care if it was raining, if it was cold, if you were hungover, or if you were sore from a hard day's work the day before. The grass had to be mowed, the weeds had to be picked, and the gardens had to be cared for. It doesn't take much for a garden to lose its beauty. It must be constantly cared for; that's why he loves meetings. They're a way to care for and cultivate your culture.

As a master landscaper, Mr. Hank reminded his team that the flowers and the grass and the bushes and the trees didn't care about their excuses. They committed to tending to the landscaping no matter what, and their commitment is what made the difference. Alex made the mistake once of brushing off the fact that a plant in a giant yard had died. *It was just one plant, and if we removed it, nobody would ever notice.* This was the wrong answer, Alex learned quickly. Every bush and every flower and every tree mattered in the yard. When one feature is not thriving, the entire yard suffers.

"We can't just simply cut the plant out, toss it away, and hope nobody notices. If we do this, there will be a very obvious void in our yard. It could take a long time to fill that space. Instead, it's important that we give that dying bush everything that it needs and all of our focus and attention see that we commit to it to grow. If it dies, at least we can say we did everything in our power to foster it," Mr. Hank said seriously. Alex never forgot this. Mr. Hank had a way to bring things back to life we thought were dead. That goes for plants and people. Some of the people on his crew were recovered addicts, and others were on parole. One summer with Mr. Hank is all it took for him to change lives. Everyone left Mr. Hank full of confidence and ready to attack the world.

Alex approached his teammates the same way. Of course, not everyone was going to work perfectly with each other. Personalities were going to clash; work styles were going to differ. But every person mattered and deserved Alex's time, attention, and investment. It wasn't good enough to just cut out an employee who wasn't thriving and replace them with someone else. Alex wanted to make sure that, at the end of the day, he could confidently say he did everything in his power and was committed to their growth, but when a weed shows up, you remove it at the root so it won't grow back.

Alex noticed Collin was unusually quiet. "You good, Collin?" Alex asked, walking over to his friend.

"I don't know, man, this whole talk about commitment really got me thinking. I was thinking about our wedding day and how we wrote these beautiful vows and how when we were standing up there in front of our friends and family, I *really* meant them. I did. Right now, I don't know, I just feel like I've messed it all up. I've completely ruined Amy's trust in me; I'm ashamed of myself. Honestly, I'm leading Jada on like there's a future, and there are a few other chicks too.

"Part of me knows that I'm not 100% committed to the law firm because it doesn't feel like what I was born to do. My whole life I had it planned out. I was going to go pro with golfing, and then when that didn't work out, I don't know. . .," Collin started walking away, and Alex followed.

"I love Amy, but I'm afraid to feel prom night all over again."

"Hey, don't beat yourself up. Just acknowledging all this today is a huge step. I know it's a lot to take in. I don't know if your marriage can be saved, but it's worth a try. It's worth changing your behavior and showing Amy that you're committed to your vows and committed to change and committed to her. And you're damn good at what you do, Collin, seriously. When it comes to your firm, you are born to lead. You may not ever get to be a pro golfer, but you could build an unstoppable team of lawyers that could help so many people. You already know the industry. You already have the people. You just have to shift the way you think about them, to embrace more of the teamwork aspect. No more of this every-man-for-himself kind of thing; it's not working," Alex said, putting his hand on his friend's shoulder. "You need to teach your lawyers everything you know and make sure they are just as confident as you."

Collin was quiet for a bit. "I've always had the mindset that either you have it or you don't. That's what I believed growing up. I was successful and loved because I was good at what I did. But that's hard to maintain. Being the best at everything and being perfect is a lot of pressure," Collin said, and Alex tried not to wince at Collin's unintentional arrogance.

"Before we came on this trip," Collin said, "Trent mentioned something about investing more time and education in our new lawyers. I hated the idea because it just meant that we were spending money and time cultivating people who weren't already good enough. It seems pointless. But after all of our talk today, I wonder if maybe I'm too hard on people. If I'm looking for perfection in others because I'm always looking for it in myself. We could start there," Collin said, finally looking at Alex. "We need to onboard better and invest in some training for our lawyers. And I'll do a meeting at least once a month, maybe once a week."

"Definitely," Alex agreed. "That would be a great place to start. And if I can help in any way, please let me know. And also, I don't want to overstep, but I know a really good couples therapist in your area," Alex said softly. Alex couldn't be sure, but he thought he saw Collin wipe a tear. Alex offered one more tidbit of advice: "You need to heal up, forgive your prom date, and move on, my man. It's not fair to Amy; she is being impacted by something that traumatized you a long time ago. Maybe you need to start therapy and work on yourself." The two of them walked back to Bobbi and Austin, who were engaged in deep conversation about women in business.

"You boys okay?" Bobbi asked, trying to read their faces. She glanced over at Alex who gave her a reassuring smile.

"I don't know about you guys, but I could be playing the best game of golf of my life," Bobbi said confidently. "You guys ready?"

Alex and Collin hopped back into their golf cart and followed the girls to the next hole. It was quiet, and this time, Collin didn't feel the need to fill the silence with unnecessary noise. At this point, Alex's golf score was the last thing on his mind. The conversations and revelations that were happening on the green were life-changing, and he was so thankful to have a front-row seat to it all. Now only one more hole to play.

Trait 6: Commitment

Take action: Think about an upcoming project, task, or idea that your team needs to complete and/or work on. Involving people in the planning and decision-making process increases their level of commitment. How will you involve your team in this planning process for this upcoming project or task?

COMMITMENT

A winning team consists of members who are completely devoted emotionally and intellectually. Because team members know why they are there and how they can help advance the cause, they are locked in and willing to do what is necessary to achieve the desired results.

12

APPROACH

The drive to the 18th hole was a quiet one. Austin was scrolling through the notes on her phone, high-lighting the parts that stuck out to her. Bobbi and Collin were quiet as they focused on navigating the golf cart down the path, and Alex was admiring the greens.

"So I guess it makes sense to end our game with Dad's final notes. You've mentioned culture a lot today and how all of the things we've discussed impact a company's culture. Your first note here is about defining company culture," Austin said, looking down at her phone.

"Culture is a set of values, beliefs, language, and pri-orities that define rules of behavior," Alex said matter-of-factly. "Your company has a culture whether you intentionally build it or not. It's what your leaders think, say, do, and believe and how that trickles down through the rest of the company.

"I was a bad leader for the first couple of years and figured it out. We didn't grow Red's until I became the solid foundational leader we needed me to be despite being dyslexic. I hid it for years, guys. I had to focus on my peo-ple; it was the only thing I did well. I needed Christy then and Shawn now to manage the numbers. Austin is keeping score today. So, I dialed into everything I learned about teamwork and everything I learned from Mr. Hank about people and plants. He wasn't good with numbers either; Mr. Hank was dyslexic too. He wasn't my biological dad, but over time it was just like I was a chip off his old block.

I see people just like a plant or a tree. And I see a collection of my teammates just like a garden or a landscape, and my job is to take care of my people. I delegated away my weakness and dialed into my strengths with people. It is not *I, me, or my*! I know at Red's Hardware, it is *us*. I need my teammates, and my teammates need me."

Austin teared up as she was so proud of her dad's courage and comfort with his strengths and weaknesses.

Every time Alex opened a new store, he dedicated a whole day to talking about company culture. He'd show pictures of iconic logos like Nike and Zappos and ask his recruits what these companies had in common. Eventually, they'd get to the answer: a strong company culture. They'd talk about how teams with a strong, positive culture have higher productivity, see lower absenteeism, lower healthcare costs, and tend to retain more employees.

When he met with the managers of a new store, he'd always ask the same questions. What is the vibe of our organization? What type of person would want to work here? What does everyone know we do well? What do we always do? What is not tolerated here? Their answers gave Alex a clear idea about the culture in each store, and if it didn't match the company's core values or intended culture, he saw it as a learning opportunity to make a change. All his regional managers and managers learned how to preach the same message.

"How would you define your company culture?" Alex asked, to nobody in particular.

"In a perfect world, I'd love to say our company culture could be described as innovative, free-thinking, creative. My dream has always been a place that felt techy but sexy, forward-thinking, and collaborative. . .," Bobbi responded.

"But?" Alex gently prodded.

"Right now it doesn't feel that way. My techs would use other words. Stifling. . .," she flinched, but then continued, "inconsistent, micromanaged. . ." she trailed off. It was clearly painful for her to admit this. Alex nodded.

"You can change the company culture, Bobbi. You can have that sexy, techy, creative, collaborative company. But it starts with you," Alex said confidently.

"And you, Collin?" Alex asked.

"Well, if we are going with our perfect-world company culture, I'd say we were professional, confident, innovative, fast-paced, influential, prominent. But right now, it feels more like unsupportive, disengaged, siloed," he said, looking down at the ground. Alex knew this was hard for both of them to admit, but he felt a huge sense of pride. Acknowledging where their company culture was right now was the first step in making the active steps toward making it what they wanted it to be.

Austin waited for a pause in the conversation and then spoke up. "Hey, this one reminds me of you, Bobbi. It says 'An athlete who reaches the top of her game doesn't suddenly coast, skipping a practice here and there or loading up on junk food once a week. She continues to push herself and her body to become even stronger.'

"What does that have to do with culture?" Collin asked.

"I'm getting there," Austin said flatly. "When we start to coast in our work habits or fail to hold each other accountable to living up to the corporate culture, cracks begin to emerge, and our culture loses its strength." She looked up at Collin, and he nodded in approval.

"Yeah, I guess that's true. When I was training for the marathon and my times were getting better and I could run farther and faster, I trained more. I ate healthier, and I paid more attention to my training. Getting faster and stronger didn't trigger me to lay off; it triggered me to put my foot on the gas and keep going"

"Exactly. We have to do this in our businesses too. Just because things are going well doesn't mean we can let go of our values or our expectations. We have to continue to be intentional about living up to our core values and ensuring that they remain the building blocks of our culture," Alex explained. "We have to constantly get bigger, stronger, and faster, especially if we want to grow.

"Another question I consistently asked my managers when we're talking about culture is 'What of your daily work habits are most closely tied to the corporate culture?' This is usually a tough question for them to answer, but it allows us to have a good conversation and identify how they are tempted to coast from time to time. We use these discussions to recommit to never being the cause of a crack in the cultural foundation. You can't let your teammates down."

Anytime he thought about culture, he thought about store #88. For some reason, this store seemed to struggle with the company culture concept. Alex wasn't sure if it was the people his managers were hiring or the regional manager themselves, but something felt different in store #88.

They had meetings and training on the Red's fundamentals of business to try to get the store realigned, but it always seemed to be drifting off-course. To get to the root of the problem, Alex flew in and spent a week with the managers and walked alongside them during the hiring process. New employees were hired and made sure they were doing it the Red's Hardware Way. Hoping this extra focus on onboarding these new hires would align everyone with the right habits and perspectives.

Once he thought that they had hired the right people, they shifted their attention to how they were handling each phase of business. Alex along with the other managers and regional managers carefully looked at the operational changes the managers had put into place to see if those were causing an unintended shift in the cultural direction. Store #88 finally got it together, and Alex was able to see a united and positive culture that resulted in improved sales and happier teammates. Alex had helped #88 get back to the fundamentals.

But it didn't happen overnight. Correcting that shift was like turning an ocean liner. The momentum was going in a very different direction, and reversing the course was not easy, but Alex knew it was possible. And not just possible, but necessary. If store #88 couldn't figure out how to adopt the company culture, it would impact the entire brand.

"It starts with communication. Communication about what's not working. Communication about destructive patterns. Communication about accountability," Alex added.

"Sounds like improving company culture requires a lot of hard conversations," Austin observed.

"Absolutely," agreed Alex. "If it's gotten to the point where your company culture is toxic to your employees and is negatively impacting your bottom line, you're going to have to have some tough conversations. And this goes back to what we talked about when we were discussing accountability. Hard conversations are good for the growth of your team, and they're easier when you remember you're just presenting the facts. You're not attacking, you're not belittling, you're not embarrassing. You're calling out things as you see them honestly and lovingly."

Bobbi shuddered. "I can list a few of those home conversations that I need to have off the top of my head. But you're right, when you frame it as a conversation about facts and expectations, it's not an attack. It's not personal."

"My challenge to you is to have those conversations the week that we get back. Make it a priority. They will respect you for it," Alex said. Bobbi nodded.

Alex taught his regional managers to incorporate their store's positive corporate culture into their quarterly goals. Along with setting clear expectations and reviewing the project plan, Alex always reminded his regional managers about the power of tapping into the positive aspects of their corporate culture to build momentum and ensure they meet their goals. His managers were taught to identify the aspects of their corporate culture that may slow their progress, to look for potential roadblocks, and to take specific steps to overcome those challenges. He empowered his regional manager to act like owners of the stores they were responsible for.

"Okay, everyone. You're going to have to pay attention to this one. Dad put stars and arrows all around it and underlined it about 100 times, so I'm thinking it's important," Austin said, smiling. Everyone looked at her expectantly.

She cleared her throat dramatically. "What if there is a discrepancy between any of your company's core values and your company culture?" Everyone looked at Alex.

"I know, it doesn't sound like world-changing information, but something about how Professor Hightail worded this stuck with me. After he told us this, he explained that an organization's culture is built on the core values being communicated and demonstrated. They're linked. They go hand in hand. You can't have one without the other. If your company does not have core values, if it does not follow its core values, or if your employees haven't bought into the core values, it' s going to negatively affect the company culture. He said this about three times. He made it a big deal and wanted us to know how important it was. Hence the arrows and the stars." Alex smiled.

"It all comes back to the name of the class, Cultivate: Business Fundamentals for Business Leaders. When an organization cultivates its core values, it builds a company culture. Just like here on the golf course. All of the different aspects of the course come together to build this stunning place where we've spent the day. As leaders, it's our job to cultivate those core values. We have to know them, share them, teach them; we have to give them the attention that they deserve, or they're just going to wither away," Alex said passionately.

"Kind of like what you were saying with your gardener friend. The guy you spent your summers with. Mr. Frank," Collin added.

"It was Mr. Hank. But thanks for listening," Alex said sarcastically. "Yes, just like that. He instilled core values in us so that we could build a successful lawn care team. We knew and understood the core values of the business and used those to do our job effectively."

Everyone took a second to take it all in. It was feeling like everything was coming full circle. All the things they talked about that day, the common goals, communication, accountability, trust, chemistry, commitment, core values, and culture: all had to be cultivated carefully for a business to succeed. It was becoming clear that those who knew the importance of their company's core values and were intentional about cultivating them were more successful and happier than those who did not.

Alex hoped that Austin could see this too. He hoped that today's conversation gave her a head start in establishing the importance of a company's core values, and that with this information she would be ahead of the game as she started her college courses and eventually stepped into the workforce.

As Austin tapped her ball into the hole for the final time, the whole group cheered. It has been a great day of golf, but more importantly, it has been a day of big conversations, self-reflection, goal setting, and self-awareness. Alex was exhausted, but he knew the day wasn't over just yet. They all knew exactly what was going to happen next. They returned to their golf carts and headed straight for the hotel's famous Flagler Steakhouse that overlooked the course. They needed to tally up the final scores to see who won.

Reflection

Are your company's/group's/team's core values being communicated and demonstrated in a way that is creating the culture you want to build?

13

MULLIGAN

13

MULLIGAN

The four tired friends followed the hostess through the busy steakhouse and out to the balcony overlooking the course. They ordered their drinks and settled in to talk about their day of golf. Surprisingly, although most of their attention was focused on business development, they all played one of their best golf games ever. They chatted quietly about their favorite part of the course, relived some of their best places, and playfully jabbed at each other over small mishaps and mistakes.

Austin read out their scores.

- Alex, 71
- Austin, 80
- Bobbi, 73
- Collin, 69

"You know, I'm so glad we did this. Our annual get-together always means so much to me, but having Austin here and having you guys really pour into her with your wisdom and experience, it's just priceless. She has been cultivated into a fine young lady. I'm so thankful for you and your years of friendship and everything you've taught me," Alex said seriously.

"Cheers to good friends, and good golf!" Bobbi said, raising her glass.

"And Professor Hightail," Alex added as they clinked their glasses together. They perused the menu and ordered swiftly when the waiter came back to their table.

"I'd also like to say that I'm really thankful for this experience. Dad, I did enjoy hanging out with you today, and Bobbi, Collin, your insight and experience mean more to me than you know. I aspire to be like you guys, and I've learned a lot today about the kind of business leader I want to be," Austin said sweetly. Bobbi wiped a tear from her eye and reached out to squeeze Austin's hand. Collin winked.

Alex sat back in his chair and looked out over the sprawling view. A lot has happened over 18 holes, and he was sure it would take him a few days to process. He wanted the best for his friends, he really did, and he hoped that today's conversations would help them to look inward and make some changes that would benefit them both personally and professionally.

The appetizers came, followed by more drinks, followed by gorgeous plates of fine ribeye steaks and food that the friends devoured with more great laughs and fellowship. When they were finished, they all said yes to the dessert menu and ordered a few things to share. Alex didn't want the day to end. He wanted to talk more about the power of teamwork, to dive deep into the strategy for cultivating core values and building great businesses. But he knew Bobbi and Collin had reached their limit and already had a lot to process and think about. He knew his friends well enough to leave it alone and focus more on the chocolate masterpiece on the table and the good people he was sharing it with.

When the check came, Alex quickly grabbed the black leather folder. He glanced down at the check, but then it started happening. The numbers looked jumbled and didn't make sense. He blinked rapidly, looked up a few times, and tried to discreetly make out the numbers so he could calculate the tip. He glanced over at Austin who was already watching him. She was used to this and was ready to jump in if he needed it. His dyslexia was the reason he failed his accounting classes and why the family budget was Christy's job. It also made it hard for him to keep score during a golf game or calculate a tip for dinner. She leaned over to help him figure it out, and Collin noticed.

"Hey, need us to pitch in?" Collin asked, reaching for his wallet.

"No, no, the dyslexia makes it hard for him to. . .," Austin trailed off. She could see in Collin's face and Bobbi's that it finally clicked, how serious his learning challenges were, how serious his learning challenges were. Alex smiled sheepishly, and Austin felt horrible. She watched Bobbi's face as it turned from confusion to realization.

"That's why you failed accounting!" she squealed, and then lowered her voice. "I could have helped you!"

"That's why you never want to keep score when we golf. Or why you are anal about hiring people who are good with numbers!" Collin said. Alex nodded.

Collin and Bobbi were astounded. They looked up to Alex and put him on a pedestal. They didn't think he had *any* weaknesses and were amazed that he was building such an empire while living with such an obstacle. Collin says, "When you mentioned it on the course, we didn't take you seriously. Wow!"

"Guys. It's not a big deal. I've learned to live with it. I've learned tools and tricks to help me work through it, and Collin, you're right. I know my weaknesses and intentionally hire people who can fill in these gaps. I wouldn't call it anal but. . .."

Austin started to apologize for bringing it up, but Alex stopped her. He was confident in himself, which meant owning his strengths and weaknesses. He was almost thankful for a chance to show Bobbi and Collin that he struggled too. With Austin's help, he tipped generously, as usual, and the group of four moved slowly through the busy steakhouse and out to the parking lot and took the shuttle back to the lobby of The Breakers.

Collin said good-bye first. "Today was a good day, guys. I usually don't get emotional, and I don't want to make this a big thing, but I really did appreciate everything we talked about today. I'm going home with a lot to think about, and I have you guys to thank for that. Austin, I do not doubt that you are going to make a name for yourself in whatever industry you choose. You've got an incredible role model, and it's already so obvious that you've got a good head on your shoulders. I can't wait to see what you do, and if you ever need a lawyer. . .," Collin said quickly, trying not to get emotional. "In fact, you should think about law school; you'd make a great lawyer."

Austin hugged him, which surprised him, but he returned the gesture. Collin pulled Bobbi into a tight hug and whispered something into her ear. She squeezed him for an extra second and then let him go and looked away. He held out his hand to Alex, who took it and pulled him in for a hug as well. "I've always looked up to you. Thank you for today," Collin whispered and then pulled away from the hug without looking at Alex. He walked toward the elevator, and all he could think about was cultivating his law firm and his marriage.

"I want you to come to Nashville," Bobbi said, turning to Austin. "I want you to come to the office and see how we do things. You can stay at my house, we can go do girly things like get our nails done and go shopping, and then we can go into the office and I can show you how to be a Boss," she started, and then looked at Alex, "a powerful woman in business," she corrected. Alex nodded.

"I would love that. You know you're my mentor now, so just let me know when!" Austin said excitedly. Austin's phone rang, and she excused herself, leaving Alex and Bobbi standing alone.

"Have those tough conversations this week. It will make all the difference. And for the love of everything holy, stop micromanaging those people. They know what to do, and you've got to give them the freedom and flexibility to do it. Don't be so scared of change. You are a smart, powerful, inspirational, creative leader, and they're lucky to have you," Alex said, looking into her eyes. She looked away.

"I mean it. Just do it. And if I can help in any way, please let me know. I'll fly out if you need me to. I want you to succeed. I want you to be able to cultivate a business that works and that you're proud of. Collin has a lot of work to do, but Bobbi, you aren't far off. I remember that first day at golf practice, you brightened up the room and you still do. Hire great people and let them brighten up their rooms without you. You're close. I feel like just by tweaking a few things that we talked about today, GolfTek could grow," he said, ignoring her obvious discomfort with the serious tone in his voice. "But you must grow first."

"Okay, okay. I will. And I know sometimes I may not seem receptive, but I really do listen to everything you say. I admire you, I admire your family, and I admire the relationship you have with your daughter. This trip is always really special to me, and I'm thankful for it."

Austin returned to the group just as Bobbi was saying her final words. "I have to head to bed, guys; I have an early flight to catch," Bobbi said, pointing to the elevator that would whisk her up to her room. "One day I'll have my own plane, Alex, just like you. And leave when I want to. . . . just like you." Bobbi wrapped Alex and Austin into one giant bear hug, and she headed up to her room for the night.

"I can't believe you saved these notes," Austin said, holding up her phone. "I really will use them. There's a lot of good stuff in there."

"I hope so," Alex replied, "I hope they help you as much as they help me."

"You may have had Professor Hightail and all of his golden nuggets of wisdom, but I think I have something better," she said.

"Oh yeah? What's that?" he asked

"You," she said, smiling. She pretended not to notice the tears welling up in her dad's eyes and hit the up button to call the elevator. The doors opened, and they stepped inside. Alex grabbed her hand and squeezed it, and they rode the rest of the way in silence.

The following days felt like a blur for everyone. Alex got right back to work managing his 150 stores, carefully tending to his yard, and taking countless trips to the store to get Austin everything she wanted for her new apartment.

During one of these trips, he got a text from Collin. He had told Amy everything, and to his complete surprise, they agreed to counseling. They were headed to their first appointment with the therapist Alex recommended, and he was optimistic about their future. He had also invested in some professional development for his new lawyers and was planning a retreat to help them cultivate a healthier and more cooperative firm.

Bobbi also filled Alex in with a few promising updates a few weeks after they parted ways at The Breakers. She had secured a second meeting with Maggie, who was open to the idea of coming back to GolfTek, under many conditions. Bobbi was working on accepting those conditions and had given Craig that well-deserved raise. She also fired Johnny because he missed his dead-line. Again.

Alex liked getting these regular updates from his friends. He loved having a front row seat to their growth and felt honored that they wanted to share their news with him. Two of his closest friends were cultivating new lives and new businesses right in front of his eyes, and nothing could make him happier. Alex was already looking for-ward to next year's trip and was hopeful that his friends would continue to focus on their people. He knew this was the secret. He knew that if they just did this, if they took what they learned on the golf course and then got out of the way, they'd experience the success they were so desperately looking for.

On Friday, Bobbi and Collin both received packages at their respective doorsteps. When they opened it, they found a small bag of soil, gardening tools, two ceramic pots, a watering can, and a handful of flower seeds.

The note was simple: *cultivate.*

redwood noun

red·wood | \ 'red- wụd

Redwoods create the strength to withstand powerful winds and floods by extending their roots outwards, up to 100 feet wide from the trunk, and living in groves where their roots can intertwine. A redwood can't grow to be the tallest tree on earth *alone*.

We all have dreams and plans, but we don't all complete the process to achieve them. We want you to dream big, have big goals, and think about those big goals as if your reality is about to happen today. Even the giant redwood trees start from tiny seeds, like the kernel of an idea you've had bouncing around inside your brain for a while. But just having a seed in your pocket will not grow a tree. It must be planted, nurtured, and cared for to come to life.

Plant goals that will help you become the best version of yourself. We can achieve our goals with the right tools, accountability, a winning mindset, and the right team. Remember: we're better together; winning is a team sport.

Are you ready to get the career you want? Are you willing to become the person you need to achieve that dream? If you are prepared to invest the required work to become the person you want to be—the person you know you can be—we are ready to help you.

Today.

EPILOGUE

At Last. . .
Here's How You Can
Execute 6 Secrets You've Learned to
Build a Championship-Caliber Team That Can
Outperform Your Competition, Plus
Achieve Big Goals!

The book *Cultivate* has revealed how your company or organization can get to the next level of success. It starts with cultivating a team mindset among each of your employees.

Walter Bond and Antoinette Bond shared the proven ideas, concepts, and insights into how you and your teammates can improve your team performance so you can become a champion in your industry and sustain competitive advantage.

Walter and Antoinette highlighted the six non-negotiable traits of a winning team through a business fable. The characters resemble real-life people you can identify with and were able to overcome big challenges and obstacles and accomplish a common goal working as a team of peak performers.

If you work for a company or organization that has been struggling to recruit, develop, and retain top talent, you now have the insight to improve your results. You can work as a team using the concepts shared in this book.

We said it before, and we'll emphasize it again. Good teamwork leads to greater success. By applying the ideas, concepts, and skills communicated throughout the book, you can turn your company or organization into a champion-caliber, peak-performing team that can dominate your industry.

Don't just think about it. You've got to execute what you've learned so you can win.

Here is your next step to start now. . .

Go to https://youriteam.com/opt-inlpiteamcultivate1/ or scan the QR code to take our *free* teamwork diagnostic to see how you score. You can also learn more on how you can build a winning team.

AUTHOR BIOS

BIO FOR WALTER BOND

Walter Bond is the co-founder of the Bond Group and iTeam Consulting Group. He creates and oversees development of the content for his speaking appearances, books, courses, audios, and videos.

Walter graduated from the University of Minnesota in 1991 where he played basketball for four years. After breaking his foot twice during his senior year, Walter thought his dream to become a professional basketball player was dead. But with the right mindset, dedication, and perseverance to be the best performer, Walter was able to fulfill his dream.

On November 7, 1992, Walter became the first ever undrafted rookie to start in a season-opening game in the National Basketball Association as a guard for the Dallas Mavericks. In addition to that incredible achievement, Walter held a rookie scoring record with the Dallas Mavericks, which stood for more than 25 years for the most points scored by a rookie in their first three games. Dallas Maverick superstar Luka Doncic just broke that record.

Walter excelled at teamwork throughout his time as a basketball star with the Dallas Mavericks, Detroit Pistons, and Utah Jazz. Though he loved playing basketball, Walter had his eye on a bigger post-professional basketball career: becoming a motivational speaker.

Walter not only reached his goal but excelled at it so much that in 2015 the Council of Peers Award for Excellence Speaker inducted him into the National Speakers Association Hall of Fame®, making him one of fewer than 200 speakers alive today to have that distinguished recognition.

Today Walter is one of the most highly coveted motivational keynote speakers, with more than 2,000 speaking appearances. Each year, 100+ companies and organizations trust him as a keynote motivational speaker, former NBA player, and bestselling author to inspire their teams to champion-level greatness.

Walter also founded and continues to build America's leading motivational training and professional development organization. He has authored numerous courses, books, audios, and videos on the professional fundamentals to become a peak performer.

Plus, he teaches thousands of entrepreneurs, executives, managers, and other employees each year on improving their mindset to overcome adversity and achieve success in pursuit of big goals. Plus, he trains his audience on developing skills to improve work performance. And most recently he developed a proprietary training program for teamwork.

The Bond Group is headquartered in Boca Raton, Florida. Companies and organizations of all sizes in many industries throughout the United States hire Bond to be their keynote speaker and buy the courses, books, audios, audios and gear produced by Walter Bond.

Walter Bond has been married to his wife and business partner since 1993. They have three adult children.

BIO FOR ANTOINETTE BOND

Antoinette Bond is co-founder and chief operations officer for the Bond Group and is the CEO of iTeam Consulting Group. Partnered with her husband and business partner Walter Bond, who is a Hall of Fame® motivational speaker, Antoinette runs the operations, builds the companies from behind the scenes, and oversees customer service. Plus, she provides one-on-one coaching to help clients take their skills to the next level for greater success.

Antoinette is an entrepreneur and certified business coach with more than 20 years of experience helping entrepreneurs, executives, managers, and other professionals reach their goals. She learned the power of entrepreneurship early in life while watching her family develop its own real estate development business in Miami, Florida.

Antoinette graduated from Howard University in 1992 with a degree in public relations management and enjoyed a successful sales career, working for Dr Pepper and Glaxo SmithKline. She also parlayed this experience and her entrepreneurial skills to own and operate a Gymboree franchise for more than five years in Minneapolis, Minnesota, and build the Bond Group, a nationally recognized corporate training and development company headquartered in Boca Raton, Florida, from the ground up.

Today she serves clients worldwide. As a detail-oriented specialist in bringing ideas from the drawing board to reality, Antoinette helps corporate clients improve their team performance. She also works with individuals, coaching them to become peak performers.

Antoinette is much more than just a coach. She's also your comrade, collaborator, cheerleader, and accountability partner, who can help you to navigate your way to greater success. She provides behind-the-scenes support that can enable you to stand out and shine with confidence!

She has been married to Walter Bond for nearly 30 years. They have three adult children. all who followed Antoinette's footsteps and attended Howard University. Antoinette is also involved in several community and philanthropic initiatives. Plus, she is a member of international organizations that include The Links, Inc., Alpha Kappa Alpha Sorority, and Jack and Jill of America, Inc.

ABOUT ITEAM CONSULTING GROUP

Walter Bond and Antoinette Bond cofounded the iTeam Consulting Group after consulting with hundreds of founders, executives, managers, and entrepreneurs in companies of all sizes and in many industries throughout the United States and abroad.

What we learned is amazing. We discovered many companies focus on hiring and training top talent at the highest levels of the company or organization. Plus, they invest in leadership training.

Yet, while these top individuals were able to do a good job, the organization often fell short in achieving their highest goals or did so much later than expected.

The reason for these failures is due to poor teamwork or, at the very least, individuals performing at a lower level than what they were capable of achieving. When added together, a team of individuals each performing at below peak level often encounters lower than desirable results.

FROM RESEARCH TO INNOVATION

As a result, we focused our attention on developing a turnkey scalable solution that could provide immediate benefits among organizations that encourage or mandate their employees to enroll and complete the program.

Our patented program helps leaders shift focus from leadership to teamwork. And it encourages leaders to communicate the core values of the organization to everyone on their team. So, you can have a "peak-performing team" that can achieve extraordinary results.

Ask yourself, have you ever witnessed a major accomplishment that did not involve a high-performing team?

Whether it's in sports, engineering, medicine, law, or any other industry, a team that performs at its peak is capable to achieve extraordinary results.

That's why we invested our time and money to develop a patented solution that we're confident can help your company or organization grow to the next level and gain competitive advantage.

HOW OUR MISSION CAN HELP YOU

Our mission is focused. iTeam Consulting Group specializes in helping companies and organizations improve team performance so you can reach your goals and improve financial results. For higher revenues. Greater profits. And superior market value.

We developed a patented training program to help train your team on the various "teamwork" skills required to perform at peak level.

Plus, we developed two tests. First, a teamwork diagnostic helps business leaders rate how well their team functions and discovers the hidden weaknesses to "team productivity."

Second, a teamwork assessment identifies how well each worker performs on the team. So, you can identify which "teamwork traits" are weak before we help you strengthen your team productivity.

It's not enough for you to focus on just leadership skills. You must first shift your mindset to focus on building your team and get everyone to know and express your core values. Then you can motivate your team for peak performance so you can achieve your highest goals.

YOUR SUCCESS FOR A PEAK PERFORMING TEAM STARTS WITH ONE STEP. . .

iTeam Consulting Group is headquartered in Boca Raton, Florida. We serve companies and organizations of all sizes in many industries. Go to https://youriteam.com/opt-inlpiteamcultivate1/ or scan the QR code to take our *free* teamwork diagnostic to see how you score and to learn more on how you can build a winning team.

INDEX